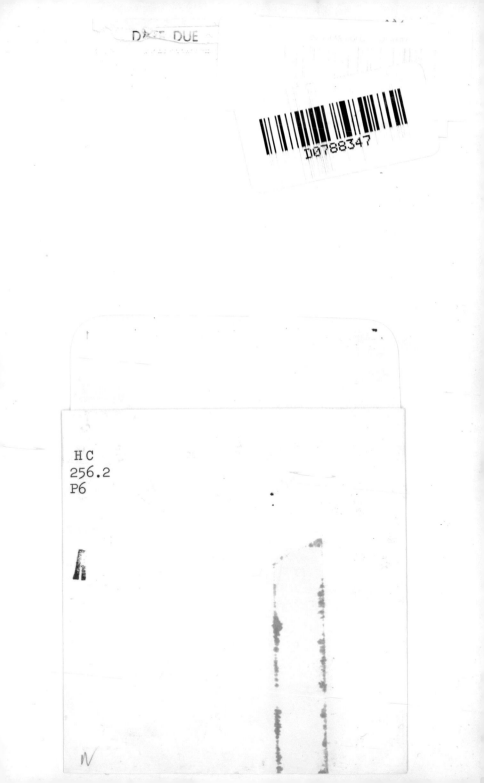

Debates in Economic History

Edited by Peter Mathias

The Gold Standard and Employment
Policies between the Wars

The Gold Standard and Employment Policies between the Wars

edited with an introduction by
SIDNEY POLLARD

METHUEN & CO LTD
11 NEW FETTER LANE LONDON EC4

First published 1970 by Methuen & Co Ltd
Introduction © 1970 by Sidney Pollard
Printed in Great Britain by
Richard Clay (The Chaucer Press), Ltd,
Bungay, Suffolk

SBN (hardbound) 416 14250 8
SBN (paperback) 416 29950 4

Distributed in the U.S.A.
by Barnes & Noble Inc.

Contents

Preface

The return to the gold standard at pre-war parity in 1925 is one of the most contentious acts of economic policy in English history, fiercely disputed at the time and a cause of disputed interpretation ever since, as Professor Pollard's introduction and this volume as a whole make clear. Reasons are not hard to seek but, as so often in historical controversies, they are fused into a double, or quadruple, compound. Disagreement exists over the results of a policy enactment seen *ex post facto*; that is, judged by hindsight using all the evidence of what subsequently happened and also information (not excluding theoretical assessments) not available to those taking decisions at the time. On these grounds, historians can claim that a policy pursued was mistaken; that other decisions would have produced more desirable results. This is not, of itself, necessarily to judge the decision-takers harshly. They could have acted 'rationally' and for the best, given the information at their disposal, in assessing *ex ante* the likely consequences. Alternatively they could be deemed to have assessed their data wrongly or acted on perverse motives, even judged according to the theoretical assumptions current in their generation. One cannot accuse a pre-Keynesian generation of Keynesian theoretical folly as fairly as one can a post-Keynesian generation, with post-Keynesian as well as Keynesian theoretical formulations in its intellectual armoury.

Disagreement remains possible at both these levels of analysis. However, the debate does not end there. Where a tradition of economic policy survives, and is still hotly debated in present circumstances, the overlay of current argument casts a long shadow over the past. Indeed, the theoretical debates over current economic policy issues are one of the important originating points for reassessments in economic history.

All these elements are present in the controversies still continuing over the return to gold in 1925; not least the post-1945 experience. The international context and the British economy since 1945 have both been very different from what they were in the inter-war period (though it is still salutary to realize that even Keynes was apprehensive of international inflationary problems in 1924). Despite this, certain structural relationships still exist, which have conditioned arguments about economic policy in a fashion providing analogues to the inter-war debate. 'Stop-go' economic management in the later 1950s and 1960s provoked arguments about whether the level of performance of the economy should always be conditional upon the preservation of a fixed parity between its currency and some external norm, be it gold or the dollar; or whether the international finance business of the City, demanding a strong pound and confidence in the currency, should be given priority over the interests of industry (both management and labour). It has been a hard lesson to learn, both now and in the inter-war years, that the strength of the pound, no less than the financial strength of the City and the services it supplies to the international economy, are integral with the efficient international performance of the economy as a whole, which determines the long-run balance of payments position.

Debate about current exchange rates – fixed, pegged, crawling or floating – with reverberations about the gold standard and parities in times past, is just now being supplemented by a wider, but related, controversy over monetary theory as a whole. In the nineteenth century these gold standard arguments were conducted in terms which invoked, as internal mechanisms, the adjustment of prices by way of exchange-rate movements, gold flows, interest-rate policy and fluctuations in the quantity of money – more particularly currency – in circulation. Although the definition of money is now more embracing and more deliberately managed techniques of control are accepted, a common core of assumptions survives that control of the quantity of money is crucial to the regulation of prices, inflation and the level of economic activity. With the new 'Chicago school' propositions now actively in current debate about the formulation of monetary policy, in monetary history may we not expect old 'currency school' formulae to be dusted off and refurbished as the old ghosts begin to walk again in new dress?

PETER MATHIAS

Acknowledgements

The editor and publishers wish to thank the following for permission to reproduce the articles listed below: Professor K. J. Hancock for 'The Reduction of Unemployment as a Problem of Public Policy, 1920–1929' (*Economic History Review*, 2nd series, XV (1962), 328–43); Dr L. J. Hume for 'The Gold Standard and Deflation: Issues and Attitudes in the 1920s' (*Economica*, new series, No. 119 (1963), 222–42); Macmillan and Co. Ltd. and Harcourt Brace Jovanovich, Inc. for 'The Economic Consequences of Mr. Churchill', from *Essays in Persuasion* (1931) by John Maynard Keynes; Professor Edward Nevin for 'The Origins of Cheap Money, 1931–1932' (*Economica*, February 1953, 24–37); Professor R. S. Sayers and The Athlone Press for 'The Return to Gold, 1925' from *Studies in the Industrial Revolution* (ed. L. S. Pressnell, London, 1960; Staples Press Ltd and Yale University Press for 'The Conflict of Opinion and Economic Interest in England' from *England and the New Gold Standard, 1919–1926* by W. Adams Brown, Jr (Yale University Press, New Haven, 1929) and George Weidenfeld & Nicolson Ltd for 'Trade Union Reactions to the Economic Crisis' (*Journal of Contemporary History*, Vol. IV, No. 4, October 1969).

Editor's Introduction

I

The First World War, it is generally agreed, represented more than an interruption in Britain's economic progress. It marked a sharp turning point, a change of direction, and, in particular, it altered substantially Britain's role in the world economy. This was partly because some adverse long-term tendencies were suddenly accelerated and telescoped in a way which made adjustment difficult, but also because the war itself created new problems.

Part of the heritage thus left by the war was the loss of some overseas investment, and the burden of vast new overseas obligations, mainly to the U.S.A., adversely affecting the annual invisible payments, which in turn reduced the capacity to make further overseas investments; the relative rise of competing foreign shipping and manufacturing industries, called into being because the supply from Britain was interrupted, particularly in formerly under-developed regions; the expansion of the heavy industries generally among all the belligerents to a size not warranted by peace-time demands; and a greatly enlarged National Debt at home. Some sectors of the economy were affected by several of these – above all the old 'staple' export industries such as coal, cotton and iron and steel, which, in any case, had shown signs of lagging in technology even before 1914. When the immediate post-war boom broke in the spring of 1920 and a severe depression set in, in Britain as elsewhere, these industries, together with shipbuilding, engineering and other export-oriented trades, were in desperate straits.

Between them they employed a large labour force and much capital, they were mostly located in geographical concentration, and not so long before they had been the foundation of British prosperity. It might have been expected, therefore, that such official fiscal and financial policy as existed would have sought to ease the pressure on them, to speed their necessary adjustment and to take account of their special problems. Nothing could have been further from the truth. A committee on post-war policy, consisting mainly of bankers but including also Pigou, the Cambridge economist, and headed by Lord Cunliffe, a former Governor of the Bank of England, had proposed in its interim report in August 1918 that the main aim of policy should be to return to the pre-war gold standard, and this proposal was repeated in its final report at the end of 1919. This was endorsed by other weighty opinion, including the Committee on Financial Facilities,[1] and after some initial misgivings[2] it became official policy. It was essentially a bankers' policy, not directly concerned with industry at all, but as it happened it required constant and sustained restriction and deflation from its inception, and therefore did grave harm to industrial capital, output and employment.

At first, during the post-war boom of 1919–20, a deflationary policy was desirable on general grounds, though it was imposed very late and mishandled in detail. But as the boom turned into depression with massive unemployment from the second half of 1920 onwards, deflationary policies continued to be pursued by the Bank of England (even after much of the Government's troublesome floating debt had been funded) and were backed by the Treasury by regular, even if not always intentional, budget surpluses.[3] These policies reduced money wages by about 40 per cent and other costs roughly in proportion, but prices at the end were still above the American level. Thus, when the decision to return to gold at the old dollar parity of $4·86 to the £ sterling was nevertheless taken early in 1925, there had already been some four years of deflation and stagnation,[4] with only the mere beginnings of a recovery in 1924.

Thus the return to gold in April 1925 had no reference to the realities of 1925, either in the field of exports or in the field of international finance. On the contrary, it was a not wholly rational attempt to recapture the power and the glory of the

---

[1] Committee on Currency and Foreign Exchanges After the War, *First Interim Report*, Cd. 9182 (1918), *Final Report*, Cmd. 464 (1919); Committee on Financial Facilities, *Report*, Cd. 9227 (1918).

[2] S. E. Harris, *Monetary Problems of the British Empire* (New York, 1931), pp. 177–80, 193.

[3] These were higher than appeared in the official presentation. E. V. Morgan, *Studies in British Financial Policy, 1914–25* (1952), p. 104.

[4] Essay 5 below.

pre-war London gold standard.[1] As far as 1925 conditions were concerned, the pound was now markedly over-valued, and in consequence exports were further discouraged and the export industries hit again, imports were encouraged, the balance of payments was adversely affected, and the pound weakened still more, so that restrictive and deflationary policies had to continue to prevent an outflow of gold and a collapse of sterling.

The result of these policies was that while the rest of the industrialized world enjoyed mild progress to 1924 and a massive boom to 1929, Britain evinced little progress, little home investment, little opportunity to switch from the older industries to the newer, and persistent mass unemployment. In turn, when the world plunged to its depression in 1929–32, Britain not only became even more depressed than she had been, still restricting credit and putting on 'the brake ... while going uphill',[2] but, having weakened her currency by the return to gold, she was one of the first countries to be attacked by international speculative capital in 1931. The U.S.A. and France, the two strongest capital markets, consented to help, but insisted that Britain pursue 'sound' fiscal policy by balancing its budget with a particular emphasis on cutting the dole for the unemployed. On this issue the minority Labour Government split in August 1931, but the new National Government could not stem the flight from sterling either and in September Britain went off gold. Instead of the catastrophe forecast by the City, there was instant relief and the headlong plunge to the depth of the depression was halted: 'the first results of the failure seemed almost entirely favourable to Britain' ... 'Its beneficial effect upon Great Britain was to some extent instantaneous and obvious.'[3] Helped along by a tariff, 'cheap money' which had now become possible, and a managed currency, the British economy was on its way to recovery within a year, well ahead of the other major industrial nations.

This picture of events would, until recently, have commanded

[1] David Williams, 'The Evolution of the Sterling System', in C. R. Whittlesey and J. S. G. Wilson (ed.), *Essays in Money and Banking in Honour of R. S. Sayers* (Oxford, 1968), pp. 280–1.

[2] R. G. Hawtrey, *The Gold Standard in Theory and Practice* (1927, 4th ed. 1939), p. 141.

[3] John Giuseppi, *The Bank of England. A History from its Foundation in 1694* (1966), p. 164; Paul Einzig, *The Tragedy of The Pound* (1932), p. x.

widespread assent.[1] In the high noon of Keynesian influence, the decade after the end of the Second World War, it became accepted, further, that Keynes's was the only voice raised against this disastrous monetary policy,[2] and he had the unusual satisfaction of seeing the solid body of the City, the Treasury and the other 'authorities' confounded, and his own views vindicated, in the years that followed. For economists this experience was of special significance, since it sharpened Keynes's mind as a necessary prelude to producing the *General Theory*, probably the most influential economic work written in this century.

After the collapse of the gold standard even the spokesmen for orthodoxy, including those whose advice had been responsible for the decision of 1925, were prepared to admit that its restoration in 1925 had been a mistake. 'I think that those who thought that the time was ripe were misled by looking too exclusively at the exchange position', Sir Josiah Stamp confided ruefully to the Macmillan Committee. 'With our present knowledge of the events which have followed 1925 it is agreed almost unanimously that the return to pre-war parity was a mistake', wrote Paul Einzig in 1932, and Lionel (now Lord) Robbins, that pillar of orthodoxy, concurred that 'in 1925 the British authorities had restored the gold standard at a parity which, in the light of the subsequent events, is now generally admitted to have been too high.'[3] In May 1932 even Montagu Norman was heard to say, 'I am now accused for having gone back to the gold standard. It was probably a mistake.'[4]

Recently, it is true, some attempt has been made to suggest that the inter-war years were by no means an economic failure, since after all the national income, and its main components, kept rising at an average annual rate of between one and two

[1] See also *Report of Committee of Finance and Industry* (Macmillan Committee), Cmd. 3897 (1931) esp. paras. 103–111, 121–5.

[2] E.g. S. E. Harris, *John Maynard Keynes* (N.Y., 1955), pp. 165 ff; Roy F. Harrod, *The Life of John Maynard Keynes* (1951), p. 357.

[3] Macmillan Committee, *Evidence*, Q. 3717; Paul Einzig, *Montagu Norman. A Study in Financial Statesmanship* (1932), p. 40, also p. 169; Lionel Robbins, *The Great Depression* (1934), p. 52. Also see T. S. Gregory, *The Gold Standard and its Future* (1931), pp. 46, 145; Henry Clay, *The Post-War Unemployment Problem* (1929), pp. 58 ff.

[4] But he added significantly, 'And still in those circumstances I would do the same thing again.' Erin E. Jucker-Fleetwood, 'Montagu Norman in the Per Jacobsson Diaries', *Lloyds Bank Review* (1968).

per cent.[1] 'Success' and 'failure' may be subjective terms and this is not the place to discuss them at length, but it will at least be agreed that we now know that modern economies can grow three times faster than the British economy did at that time; that they can employ even the 'hard core' of $1-1\frac{1}{2}$ million permanently unemployed and prevent the associated widespread destruction and waste of capital; and that they can show some growth every year instead of concentrating it (as in the later 1930s, under a new monetary policy). There was therefore at least 'failure' to do better, for which monetary policy was responsible in part. As the Minority Macmillan Report[2] put it: 'If we can do what we are doing with nearly a quarter of our industrial resources idle, what might we not do if they were all employed?'

II

There is, however, a more serious challenge to the Keynesian view from a different direction, and it also raises several other questions which it will be worth our while to pursue. This is the attempt to show that the decision to deflate in order to return to gold at the old parity in 1925, though it turned out badly, was a justifiable one to take at the time. R. S. Sayers's essay, reprinted here (Essay 4), though written some time ago and without the benefit of details recently brought to light, is still one of the best; other important contributions have been made by A. J. Youngson and the late Henry Clay.[3] Their defence may be summarized under four headings. First, the official decision to return to gold enjoyed almost universal support, and no one with any experience or authority, apart from Keynes, offered any alternative policy. Secondly, there was at that time no way of estimating correctly the price gap between Britain

---

[1] J. A. Dowie, 'Growth in the Inter-War Period: Some More Arithmetic', *Econ. Hist. Rev.* 21 (1968), and the earlier writings by D. H. Aldcroft and H. W. Richardson cited therein. Also G. C. Allen, 'Economic Progress, Retrospect and Prospect', *Econ. Journal* 60 (1950). But see Neil K. Buxton 'Economic Progress in Britain in the 1920s: A Reappraisal', *Scottish J. of Political Economy* 14 (1967).

[2] This was the *Additional Report*, signed by Bevin, Keynes, McKenna and three others, para. 53.

[3] A. J. Youngson, *Britain's Economic Growth, 1920–1966* (1967) esp. the Appendix, 'Economic Thought and Policy Between the Wars'; and Henry Clay, *Lord Norman* (1957). Also some of the reviews of Boyle's critical biography of Norman, esp. T. E. Gregory's in the *Lloyds Bank Review*.

and the U.S.A., and even today there is no agreement on whether it was nearer 10 per cent, as Keynes suggested, or $1\frac{1}{2}$ per cent, as the Chamberlain–Bradbury advisory committee guessed in its more optimistic moments. Thirdly, monetary factors had a minor influence on the depression, which was mainly due to the long-term and cyclical difficulties of industry. Fourthly, any possible positive outcome of the decision was thwarted by a number of unforeseen or unforeseeable adverse actions by others: these included the failure of U.S. prices to rise after April 1925 (which would have allowed Britain to dispense with deflation); the decision of France, Belgium and other countries to return to gold in the following years at an under-valuation of their currencies, thus snatching an unfair advantage over the pound; and the failure of British money wages to come down to the level demanded by the monetary policy, so that British prices remained too high.

The first point comes truly with an ill grace. For did not the City, and its spokesman, the Bank of England, continuously insist that it was superior in skill and ability to any other institution in the world, and that the advice from outsiders, such as Keynes, should be ignored as lacking practical experience and insight? In the contemptuous words of Montagu Norman to Churchill, in February 1925, 'In connection with a golden 1925, the merchant, manufacturer, workman, etc. should be considered (but not consulted any more than about the design of battleships).'[1] Quite apart from this, however, it is patently untrue that no protest or alternative existed. Four of the essays reprinted here give details of some of the opposition.[2] To be sure, no objection was heard from the purely overseas section of the City, but it was continuous and widespread for the whole period of this policy, 1921–31, among industry and its spokesmen, among labour organizations, among politicians, even among those joint-stock bankers who took an interest in industry, and among one or two directors of the Bank of England itself. The Mond–Turner Conferences, which were in part responsible for the Macmillan Committee, made the protest

---

[1] Quoted in D. E. Moggridge, *The Return to Gold, 1925. The Formulation of Economic Policy and its Critics* (Cambridge, 1969), p. 49. This is the latest, and much the best-informed account of this episode.

[2] Essays 2, 5, 6 and 7 below.

against the gold standard one of their main concerns. The Bank
of England was well aware of the widespread opposition, and
Norman himself and the advisers of the official Committee on
the Currency and Bank of England Note Issues,[1] who were
mainly responsible for inducing Churchill to return to gold in
1925, were inclined, even as late as the end of 1924, to postpone
the step because the gap between the pound sterling and the
dollar was still too wide. The final plunge was due to a con-
junction of several almost accidental factors, including the
Conservative election victory, the speculative rise of the exchanges anticipating return at the old par, and the mischance
that of the four experts to whom Churchill confided his last
serious misgivings, three (Norman, Niemeyer and Bradbury)
were the most fanatical and thoughtless advocates of the gold
standard to be found anywhere in the country. Hawtrey alone
among the four was cautious. Return at less than full parity,
which it is alleged had never been seriously considered, had in
fact been frequently discussed, as for example in the authoritative
report by four leading economists to the British Association in
1921. The economists were Clapham, Guillebaud, Lavington
and Dennis Robertson. Keynes, it will be noted, was not among
them, but neither was the pliant Pigou, nor that valiant defen-
der of the banking system, T. E. Gregory.[2] The notion that no
significant protest or alternative existed in 1924–5 is a tribute
to the myth-making power of the City of London.

The second issue – the extent of the over-valuation and the
necessary deflation – has been the subject of a long and learned
controversy. Fortunately, we do not have to concern ourselves
with it here, for irrespective of the actual percentage rate, it
has always been clear, particularly to the Bank of England
itself, that the par in April 1925 did not represent a purchasing
power parity, no matter how measured, but was artificial, induced by bull speculators on sterling. Further, it has not been
disputed that the exchange after 1925 could be held only by
constant restrictive policies by the Bank, including an embargo
on foreign lending from time to time, until unemployment and

---

[1] *Report*, Cmd. 2393 (1925).
[2] British Association, *Monetary Policy, being the Report of a Sub-Committee on Currency and the Gold Standard* (1921). In 1922 the *Economist* also supported the return at a lower parity.

depression would force British workers to accept lower wages, and British industrialists to accept lower prices.

The third point, that industry was already depressed, is surely not a statement for the defence, but for the indictment. It is precisely because of the difficulties of British industry (particularly among the export trades which would be hardest hit by the return to gold on the terms chosen) that the critics' case is so strong.

The fourth type of argument has been the most widely canvassed. It is that all would have been well for the Bank of England and the Treasury, if the Americans, the French, the Belgians, sundry other nations, and the British trade unions had not behaved unreasonably or unpredictably. It is a complex argument, but unfortunately there is space to deal with it only very briefly.

Was it reasonable to expect a price rise in the U.S.A. in 1925 for the convenience of the British gold standard?[1] The answer is clearly in the negative. Federal Reserve policy throughout the twenties had been to keep prices steady, even during times of heavy gold influx.[2] In the event, the British return was followed by a slight fall of world prices which made the extent of the necessary British deflation correspondingly greater. When it is remembered that wheat and cotton, which were among the main carriers of the price fall, were also among the main British imports, the belief that the British deflation itself was a cause of the world deflation becomes plausible, though it has been strongly contested.[3]

The French and the Belgians, together with several other countries which followed their example, returned to gold after the British. In their case, however, they under-valued their currencies, thus greatly benefiting their export industries and their balances of payments. The resultant accumulation of gold

[1] Throughout, the Bank of England assumed with touching faith that it should be the policy of all other Central Banks to smooth its own path back to gold.

[2] Indeed, the perennial British complaint in the twenties was that the Americans 'sterilized' their gold, refusing to let it affect the price level in an upward direction, though this, in turn, has been denied by many American spokesmen.

[3] Macmillan Committee Report, *Evidence*, R. G. Hawtrey, QQ. 4204–6, Pigou, Q. 6088, Sir Otto Niemeyer, Q. 6698. W. A. Brown, *The International Gold Standard Reinterpreted 1914–1934*, (N.Y., 1940), pp. 795–7. Sir Charles Morgan-Webb, *Ten Years of Currency Revolution* (1935), p. 116. Henry Clay, *The Post-War Unemployment Problem* (1929), pp. 72–3.

in France, and the growing indebtedness of London to Paris after 1926, substantially contributed to the undermining of the gold standard in England. It has been alleged that no matter to what level the British returned, these nations would have undercut our exports by returning at a lower level, and if Britain had attempted to deal with that threat by waiting to let them return to gold first, the world would never have gone back to gold at all. Now all this, if true, was surely an argument either for insisting on a joint and agreed return to gold, or, if that proved impossible to negotiate, for putting sterling on gold in a position of strength rather than of chronic and incurable weakness.[1]

Finally, it has been said that all would have been well if only home prices, and particularly British wages, had come down smoothly by the full 10 per cent or whatever was necessary to reach the world price level. This issue, rightly, has always been the most bitterly contested in the debate about the gold standard. After the passage of over forty years, one is still struck by the sheer impudence of the demand by the City advisers that tens of thousands of large wage contracts should be refought and renegotiated; that inevitably in the process the weak (and the unsheltered industries) should have their wages further reduced as against the strong; that loss of profits, bankruptcies and unemployment should be deliberately provoked; and that incomes should further be redistributed from the active and the poor, to the inactive rich (the bondholders) – and all so that 'Britain' should have the satisfaction of pretending that the war had not damaged the pound sterling. It was this aspect of the decision that led to the loudest protests by trade unions and labour organizations, by industrialists and their bankers, and by politicians and economists throughout the years 1925–31.

Perhaps the most interesting facet of these arguments under our fourth heading, when used by and on behalf of those who were responsible for the fatal decision, is the eagerness with which they made professional incompetence their excuse. The advice to return to gold was given, not in the abstract but in the conditions of the day, particularly by Montagu Norman who

---

[1] T. E. Gregory argued ingeniously that return at a lower parity might have led to a boom and high employment, but that boom, like all others, would inevitably have ended and turned into a slump, so that it was better to have the depression right away. *The First Year of the Gold Standard* (1926), pp. 20–2.

always insisted that he had no theory, but dealt with 'particular market situations which were never quite the same.' The City and the Treasury advisers, drawing large incomes and enjoying power and prestige while the victims of their policy were on the dole, not only failed to do what they were paid to do – namely to foresee the likely consequences – but later made this failure their main excuse. It is not unreasonable to assume that, rightly or wrongly (and we show below that we believe, wrongly), they insisted on that explanation of professional incompetence because they felt any alternative explanation to be even more discreditable to themselves.

III

If, then, this particular revision of the classical Keynesian view of the matter has little to recommend it, there are two others which are entitled to much more respect. One, that Keynes was by no means alone in his opposition, has been discussed above. The other is to examine critically the view, fostered assiduously by Keynes himself, that what divided him from the orthodox City men was purely intellectual insight: if only he could make his theoretical argument convincing, he would persuade them to follow his alternative practical proposals also.

For someone like Keynes, brought up and living within an academic environment, the doctrine that men act out their roles of economic or political power by purely intellectual conviction, irrespective of personal involvement, was perhaps an understandable one to hold. Moreover, there was enough in his own experience with bankers and City Editors to justify his repeated and bitter denunciation of their lack of understanding.[1] It began in the very first days of war in August 1914, when he found the joint-stock banks scurrying for cash and refusing to pay it out, thus acting not only selfishly and unpatriotically, but stupidly beyond credence. In a series of bitter articles he

[1] E.g. 'It is typical of the silliness and utter lack of intellectual standards by which this controversy is carried on by City Editors . . .' (*Morning Post*, 1 August, 1925); 'The worst of the controversy, is that nine-tenths of it is carried on by people who do not know the arguments on either side' (*The Times*, 20 March, 1925). 'How can it be possible for one who knows so little what he is talking about [as Mr Churchill] to govern our course wisely?' (*New Republic*, 2 June, 1926). Harrod also records that Keynes was skilful in making visiting bankers and businessmen appear as fools at his Monday evening meetings in the early 1920s.

wrote on that occasion, he defended the sharpness of his criticism by his former admiration for the banks.[1] While the Bank of England, according to Keynes, came out well in the episode,[2] which made Cunliffe's reputation and got him his peerage, it was found soon after to give incompetent and misleading advice on such questions as the terms of the War Loans. In 1917 followed the astonishing episode when Lord Cunliffe, by then the unchallenged dictator of the Bank of England, engaging in a petty vendetta against some Treasury officials (including Keynes), attempted to block the Chancellor of the Exchequer's access to the gold held in Canada, and intercepted the letter written to the Chancellor in consequence by the American agents. Though bravely supported by his friends in the City against the wrath of Bonar Law (still inadequately recognized as perhaps the only Chancellor in this century to have stood up to the Bank), Cunliffe had to be voted off the Governorship. He reappeared in Keynes's field of vision in 1919–20 as a British Reparations Commissioner and one of the leaders of the fanatical and senseless high reparations school of thought. Again, what Keynes found unforgivable was for Cunliffe to have forgotten his professional knowledge and to have failed to recognize the insoluble transfer problem in vindictive reparations.

Moreover, although bankers are generally rich and powerful, it has always been possible to hold, with Adam Smith, that their activity requires less knowledge, and more routine, than that of almost any other business. The Bank of England itself, it should not be forgotten, had been managed on a part-time basis by its Governor, holding office for two years at a time, right up to the war, and Montagu Norman's breakthrough, becoming what was in effect a full-time Governor for twenty-

[1] 'The Prospect of Money, November 1914', *Econ. J.*, 24 (1914), p. 633; also 'War and the Financial System, August 1914', ibid; and 'The City of London and the Bank of England, August 1914', *Quarterly J. of Economics*, 29 (1914).

[2] Not everyone agreed. Paul Einzig, in a famous passage, castigated the Bank of England for its 'bank rate worship', which made it raise its rate pointlessly to 10 per cent, plunging 'the London market into a crisis far more severe than that experienced by weaker financial markets'. On the Bank's scales, 7 per cent was appropriate to a crisis, hence 10 per cent to an outbreak of war and 'the pundits of Threadneedle Street would probably have attempted to cope with the collapse of the Universe by raising the bank rate to 100 per cent.' *Economic Problems of the Next War* (1939), pp. 12–13.

four years (1920–1944) was due in large measure to the fact that at the critical dates of 1916 and 1922, he alone among the directors (being without a firm of his own since he had quarrelled with his partners) was prepared to work full time, and indeed fanatically hard, for the central institution.[1] Norman began to build up a professional and intelligence service within the Bank in the 1920s, but it would be permissible to hold that up to 1914 Central Banking in Britain was in the handicraft, rather than the scientific stage of its development, and in the 1920s it was, at best, in transition. In part, the argument over a 'managed currency' as against the gold standard turned on this question.[2] Norman and his associates always stressed that they abjured theory and went by feel, and to a large extent they were right. Their market, the credit market, was basically irrational, reacting to apparently similar phenomena once in one way, and once in another, and it would not have done to approach such an unstable, 'other-directed' world of fear and rumour and mass psychosis with a purely rational apparatus of thought.

Thus Keynes had plenty of reasons for approaching the controversy as an intellectual one, and for believing that the opposition to him was due purely to faulty thinking, or perhaps to limited thinking, orthodoxy deeming certain matters as fixed; e.g. the primacy of stable exchanges, which Keynes was willing to consider as variable. But he was wrong. Where their own interest was concerned, the bankers and City merchants showed no lack of understanding or willingness to experiment. If they disagreed with him, it was not only because they failed to follow his truths at an intellectual level; it was because they did not want to follow them, since their interests, their priorities and their aims were totally different from those of Keynes, and, for that matter, from those of the large majority of the British population.

IV

The decision of the monetary authorities in this period cannot become fully intelligible until it is realized that they were

[1] Francis Williams, *A Pattern of Rulers* (1965), pp. 200–206; Giuseppi, pp. 147–9.
[2] *Macmillan Committee Report*, para. 9.

dominated by a narrow section of the City, the section concerned with international finance, both long-term and short-term, and by its spokesman and representative, the Bank of England. No matter how ingenious and how valid its attempts might have been to present policies favourable to itself as policies favourable to the national interest, this section, like all other special interest groups in the economy, was primarily concerned with fostering its own specific advantages. Conversely, no matter how misguided and foolish its policies appear, when viewed from the national point of view, we shall fail to recognize their basic rationality if we forget whose interests they were meant to serve. This does not mean that the City was peculiarly lacking in public spirit: on the contrary, by the rationale of modern capitalism every man in business is expected to look after his own interest first. Even if some men in the City might be willing, individually, to forgo their comfort and their incomes, they would be propelled forward by the self-sustaining convictions of their whole normal environment, and by the powerful and venerated tradition in London which had always given the City the main say in the financial and monetary policy of the country.

The Cunliffe and Bradbury Committees, setting the course for policy, had been mainly committees of bankers. The Macmillan Committee, right at the beginning of its evidence, attempted to probe into the almost complete personal identification of the Court of the Bank of England with the extremely narrow sector of overseas finance, but it was too easily put off by the half-truths of the Deputy Governor, Sir Ernest Harvey, who pretended that it was changing significantly. Perhaps he was thinking of the (internal) Revelstoke Committee which proposed in February 1918, that 'in view of the narrowing field of choice for candidates of the time-hallowed mercantile type, members of British banks with branches in India, the Colonies and South America should be considered eligible'.[1] Joint-stock bankers, and the home Discount Market, let alone industrialists, would of course continue to be excluded. Some changes were made afterwards, but in fact, in 1924–5, of the twenty-six members of the Court including the Governor, at least fifteen

[1] Macmillan Committee, *Evidence*, Harvey, QQ. 96–110; Guiseppi, p. 143; Clay, *Norman*, p. 107.

were connected with that narrow section of overseas banking, and five with shipping and insurance; only two at most could be described as industrialists. Keynes, who always maintained that 'one of our greatest industries was international banking', was very unsympathetic to E. F. Wise of the I.L.P. who in his evidence to the Macmillan Committee urged that the Bank of England should be made more representative and cease to be a 'self-appointed corporation' because

> from the circumstances of the composition of the Bank, from its traditional closer relations to the City of London than to the problems of employment and of industry, it is biased in favour of the City rather than of industry. . . . The monetary policy in the last few years . . . has paid much more attention to the special interest of the City of London as an international money market than to the interests of industry and employment in this country, and . . . a Council constituted as I have contemplated, would, and should, put the interests of employment and of industry above the interests of the money market.[1]

Keynes was not impressed, and held to his quixotic views of how political decisions are arrived at:

> All this discussion in regard to alteration of the machinery is, in the actual world in which we are living, very academic. The difficulty was, and is, first of all to decide what is wise, and then, having reached some sort of idea about that, to persuade the people who matter, and whose opinion is worth having, to reach unanimous agreement that that is right.[2]

The representatives of the City themselves, and notably Norman and Harvey of the Bank, and Hopkins of the Treasury, had no doubt that their policies were concerned solely with the gold reserve, with exchange rates and exchange facilities and similar matters, and not at all with Keynes's priorities such as employment or output, though they learned quickly after 1925 to build up defences against the powerful interests outside the City whom they were damaging so grievously. This is clear from every line of their evidence to the Macmillan Committee, and indeed from all the surviving documents and expressions of the period.

[1] QQ. 7152, 7082, 7187, *passim.*   [2] Ibid. Q. 7214.

Among the thousands of diary entries referring to [Norman's] many and varied cares of office, there are less than half a dozen oblique allusions to the specific problems of domestic unemployment and industrial stagnation. By and large, Norman believed himself to be above such issues.[1]

Traditionally, bank rate and open market policy, and even currency and fiscal policy, had been concerned with money market equilibria only, and policy-makers and their advisers were puzzled, angry and resentful when asked to take into account the problems of coal-mining or cotton spinning. The leaders of banking opinion simply took it for granted that their pound sterling must be fixed first, and all else adjust to it. They cut a poor figure before the Macmillan Committee, and Norman's evidence had to be heavily edited and censored, not because they lacked a 'correct' theory, but because they were made to pretend to consider priorities that had never in fact entered into their decision-making.

The defence could be made, and it has been made most persuasively, perhaps, by Henry Clay in his biography of Norman, that behind the apparent concern for the sole welfare of the City, there was the assumption that only with a sound currency and exchange could industry flourish, so that Norman was as public-spirited as his critics, and merely believed in different means of reaching the same goal. Harvey, Deputy Governor of the Bank, put at the end of his list of Bank objectives, 'I may be asked . . . do we not pay attention to the condition of trade? I say that if the machine is functioning properly the condition of trade should be reflected in the factors to which I have referred.'[2]

This view, standing Keynes on his head, is at first sight attractive and plausible. After all, there has never been a sectional interest which has not believed its private benefit to coincide with national prosperity, and that what is good for General Motors is good for the nation, though few have ever had their hands on the tiller as long as the City of London. Unfortunately, it cannot survive a moment's investigation. The link between the Bank's policies and the economic losses and stagnation which they caused were known and, reluctantly,

[1] A. Boyle, *Montagu Norman* (1967), p. 142, also 196–204; Clay, *Norman*, pp. 135, 166–7; Paul Einzig, *Montagu Norman* (1932), pp. 52–3, 217.
[2] Macmillan Committee, *Evidence*, Q. 7512.

acknowledged by Norman himself. And the suggestion that for at least ten years (1921–31) a policy was pursued and would have continued longer if it could have been done, in ultimate favour of a beneficiary who meanwhile was patently suffering and collapsing from its effects, is straining credulity too far. It is surely more reasonable to believe that the policy was designed for the sake of the interests which its sponsors said they intended to benefit, and which in actual fact they did, for the time being, benefit. Even if this ultimate, but primary concern for industry had been true, however, it would have shown only that the City suffered from the foolish egocentricity of the fly on the rim that thought it made the wheel go round. The City's prosperity was always based, ultimately, on Britain's industrial strength, and not the other way about. By undermining industry (particularly exports) the City cut the ground from under its own feet, in the long run. While the bankers were fond of boasting that the difference between their priorities and those of industry derived from the fact that industry thought in terms of short runs while they took the long view, the exact opposite was the case: for the sake of their own short-term advantage, they foolishly damaged both their own and the national interest in the long run.[1]

An extraordinary amount of ink has been spilt describing the greatness and vital importance of the City and banking business for which, allegedly, an early return to the fixed exchange rates of the gold standard at the old parity was vital, at no matter what cost to the rest of the economy. In fact, the section of the City affected was remarkably small. Experience in Britain and abroad had shown that a managed currency with fluctuating exchanges did no harm to industry, to overseas trade, even to genuine (as distinct from speculative) capital exports. Much of the banking, insurance and shipping business would remain prosperous as long as industry was prosperous. The most diligent search to find underneath the mound of verbiage any concrete examples of the type of firm that did need the old gold standard, the country's 'international prestige' (the word prestige was used more than any other), for its prosperity, has come up with a remarkably thin list. One hears of 'international banking', of a 'free market for currencies and

[1] Clay, *Norman*, p. 155; Moggridge, pp. 48, 88.

. . . for securities', of international short-term lending and of the commissions and profits made on bills and on the exchanges – but even here Sir Robert Kindersley, one of the most vociferous advocates of the gold standard, had to admit that in his firm, Lazard Bros., a large proportion of the profits accrued to its French owners.[1] Apart from this, creditors and bond holders would benefit by deflation as such. All the evidence supports the Macmillan Committee's conclusion that no matter how valuable their gains, 'it is not likely that they have gone even a fraction of the way towards compensating for the losses of wealth through unemployment in recent years.'[2]

It is not now possible to determine whether any of the men of the City were at all troubled by the ethics of their position, whether there was ever an echo of that powerful and humane memorandum written by Churchill to his advisers in February 1925, deploring the sacrifices imposed on the country by a handful of rich and influential men. But whether induced by hidden moral qualms, or by a realization of the poverty of their theoretical arguments,[3] it is a curious fact that the bankers frequently used a moral terminology for their decision. This had two broad aspects. One was the common, almost pathological, preference of bankers and Treasury men for cuts, restrictions and sacrifices, as if they had some independent merit of their own.[4] This was a repeated complaint by Keynes. Norman was by no means the only Central Banker who was hoping for a gold drain so that he could persuade his Govern-

---

[1] Macmillan Committee, *Evidence*, QQ. 1193 ff. When discussing the temporary embargo on overseas issues in 1924–5, Norman stated that it affected 'a small body of people, all very well known to us, and known to one another.' Q. 3424.

[2] Para. 252.

[3] 'Many conservative bankers regard it as more consonant with their cloth, and also as economizing thought to shift public discussion of financial topics off the logical on to an alleged "moral" plane, which means a realm of thought where vested interests can be triumphant over the common good without further debate.' Keynes, *A Tract on Monetary Reform* (1923), p. 75.

[4] 'The recent [1924] agitation for a "little" inflation to remove the industrial depression,' one Puritan Scotswoman believed, 'shows the moral degradation which has spread through certain classes of the community.' Mary Theresa Rankin, *Monetary Opinion and Policy, 1924–34* (1935), p. 24. The much maligned 'economic man' of the early nineteenth century, she went on vigorously, if unhistorically, 'accepted the consequences of his follies, worked hard and paid his debts. The prices of his goods did not include the cost of the Napoleonic War'. p. 117.

ment to impose tighter restrictions.[1] But in the course of the argument over the return to gold, when Sir Charles Addis spoke of the 'sacrifice [that would not be] too high a price to pay', or when Sir Robert Kindersley urged that 'we have got to take our medicine, and I believe that it is healthy that we should',[2] the sacrifice and the medicine were to be the lot of the miners and shipbuilders, the entrepreneurs and the unemployed. The speakers using the high moral tone, however, would be among the small number of beneficiaries. Further, the morally desirable business losses and bankruptcies were to have the alleged advantages of revealing hidden weaknesses. One of the most bizarre examples of this was Bradbury's statement at the famous dinner disputation arranged by Churchill before the return to gold: by raising British export prices artificially, he maintained, the gold standard would force Britain to stop 'living in a fool's paradise of false prosperity', and make her export industries more competitive.[3]

The second aspect of this stress on morals was the alleged superiority of banking over politics, and the consequent unwillingness to trust politicians with the economic fortunes of their peoples. It derived partly from the experience of inflation during and after the war, which was put down to political chicanery rather than to the war. Out of it arose the moral denunciation of the 'managed currency' of 1914–25, and the dangerous myth that a gold standard like the one of 1925–31 was automatic, and not (as it in fact was) also 'managed', but managed in the interest of a small sector of the economy only. Out of it also arose the persistent attempt by Montagu Norman to form a kind of 'International' of Central Banks which would by-pass the politicians in the interest of 'sound' finance. He failed because in no other country did the Central Bank enjoy the independence from, let alone dominance over, the responsible political authority which was enjoyed by the Bank of England.

But while we may agree that some doubts exist as to the trustworthiness of politicians, it is by no means clear that trust in the Bank of England under Montagu Norman would have

---

[1] E.g. Clay, *Norman*, p. 116; Paul Einzig, *World Finance 1914–1935* (1935), p. 122; Clarke, pp. 100–1.

[2] Moggridge, pp. 27–8; Macmillan Committee, *Evidence*, QQ. 1656–7;

[3] Sir John Grigg, *Prejudice and Judgment* (1948), p. 183.

been wholly justified either: as the episode of 1917 had shown, one of the weaknesses of the Bank was that it could not even be trusted to control its own Governors. Autocratic, irresponsible and frequently incompetent as Cunliffe was, his Committee of Treasury (when he chose to tell them what he was doing in the Bank's name) yet supported him in his struggle for power with the Government, even in the critical war year of 1917 when all other interests had to be subordinated to the War Cabinet, and they did this because of their conviction that the Bank's authority should never be subordinate to the Government. Even Cunliffe's successor as Governor, the weaker Cokayne, defied the Government with impunity over a bank rate decision while the nation was still at war.

Nor were the Directors apparently able to end the reign of Montagu Norman which began in 1920, though even on his own terms, abstracting from the public interest and judging him only by the aims he set himself, his career must surely rank as one of the most complete failures in public life in this century. His often-stated aim was to make London a successful, leading and powerful financial centre; to keep the pound sterling strong and stable; and to maintain the independence of the Bank, if possible in a leading role in an association with other similarly constituted Central Banks.

With these ends in view, he heartily approved the American loan settlement in 1922–3, though it proved much more harsh than any other settlement that the Americans were later willing to sign, and placed a severe burden on the British exchanges for the next twelve years. But it was considered a worthwhile sacrifice to gain American support for the planned British gold standard. Norman frittered away badly-needed foreign exchange in setting up Central Banks in the Austrian successor states and other European countries, which may have increased his own sense of importance but was to contribute to the weakening of sterling later; and in 1925 he led England back to gold on a parity which permanently weakened London as a world financial centre, and, because of the effects of high rates on activity and public opinion at home, reduced the Bank's freedom of manoeuvre. Throughout the 1920s, and for reasons which are not entirely clear but may well have been purely personal, he attempted to favour Germany and to thwart the

French, which was not only frequently in conflict with Foreign Office policy, but, much more seriously, meant that he had good relations with the centre of weakness which helped to drag down the pound in the summer of 1931, but was on bad terms with the single centre of strength which could have assisted London. From 1927 onwards the accumulation of gold and sterling assets by the French (who had pursued a policy opposite to his own and had thereby acquired both full employment and a very strong currency[1]) put London totally at the mercy of the Banque de France, which did not deter Norman from continually provoking its Governor. His characteristic and almost unbelievably foolish move to support Austria in 1931 was intended to defy the French, who were willing to help Austria on their terms, but instead it set off the avalanche which finally engulfed and sank the pound.

We have already seen that the return to gold in 1925 was a gamble on certain developments abroad and at home which did not come off; but Norman added to this cardinal sin of bankers, the unsuccessful gamble with his clients' assets, yet another – the living on borrowed fugitive money. The gold standard parity had so weakened the balance of payments, that Britain could survive only by attracting short-term loans by high interest rates (which in turn inhibited enterprise at home) and it was these funds which, by their flight (induced in turn by sterling's weakness under the gold standard), made the collapse of 1931 inevitable.[2] In 1930 Norman refused a French loan which would have funded some of these short-term loans, as he refused to recognize the fact of his own weakness and of French strength. Every account of that final collapse notes the famous telegram of the New York bankers on the fatal 23 August, 1931 when the Labour cabinet split. In this telegram New York demanded to know whether the City and the Bank of England were satisfied with the proposed budgetary cuts, before judging whether a further dollar loan to bolster the pound sterling would be forthcoming, and it was this demand which led to

[1] 'Today', Paul Einzig, an admirer of Norman, commented ruefully in 1932, 'everybody is aware that a devaluation of sterling would not have prevented the recovery of London's position as a banking centre. The example of Paris duly proves this.' *Tragedy of the Pound*, pp. 28–9.

[2] J. H. Jones, 'The Gold Standard', *Economic J.*, 43 (1933); Gregory, *Gold Standard*, p. 49, and *First Year*, p. 91.

the charge of a 'bankers' ramp'. But few have noted that on that very same date G. L. Harrison, of the Federal Reserve Bank, and a friend of England in New York, also got in touch with Norman, then in Canada, who was too 'ill' to attend at the Bank, but not too ill to sabotage his own Government by advising the Americans that the proposed cuts were insufficient, and insisting that the plight of sterling was an excellent opportunity of ensuring 'that the program . . . must be sufficiently drastic to place the cost of output and wages on a competitive basis with the rest of the world.'[1] Thus even at that desperate stage Norman still thought of drastic cuts and adjustment over the whole economy – all for the sake of preserving his dollar exchange rate.

Thus in just over ten years of this rake's progress, London had been reduced from the most powerful European financial centre by far, disputing the lead with New York, to a weak, dependent and insecure money market, a symbol of failure and default. Even the City, in the end, had lost out by having its narrow interests protected too selfishly. Yet that poor, tortured, and mentally unstable Governor, notoriously unable to collaborate with anyone on equal terms, going 'ill' whenever the difficulties brought on by his policies caused a crisis, inarticulate as to his ideas and a resounding failure as to his practice, was not dismissed but stayed on for another thirteen years, until he was forced to resign solely for medical reasons in 1944. It is hardly conceivable that a political leader could have got away so easily with such a massive failure, and the fact that Norman did does not increase one's trust in the Central Banks as against the politicians.

To complete the record, it remains to be added that the British monetary authorities were slow to make use of the relief afforded by a freely-floating exchange rate after September 1931: a 6 per cent bank rate was kept on for several months and Norman was afraid it might lead to an 'unwarranted credit expansion' – at the bottom of the slump.[2] But they soon learned

---

[1] Clarke, p. 211.

[2] Einzig, *Norman*, p. 159. Robbins, as ever an extremist in the support of outdated ideas, went even further. 'If we are to avoid inflationary disturbances,' he thundered in *Lloyds Bank Monthly Review* for October 1932 (!) the authorities in different financial centres must work the gold standard on lines much more

to operate the Exchange Equalization Account and, having established a cheap money policy for other purposes, kept it as a general stimulus to trade.[1] The City appeared, from time to time, unhappy about the success of devaluation, and hankered after a renewed gold standard with its restrictions, notably during the World Economic Conference of 1933, and it must be confessed that the Treasury, as ever reflecting the needs of the City rather than of the country, supported this even more vigorously. But the powerful interests now temporarily massed against such a course,[2] as well as its innate defiance of common sense, prevented it being taken too seriously.

V

The emphasis placed here on the specific self-interest of a section of the City as an explanation of financial policy in 1921–31 does not require a crude assumption that everyone in public life simply feathers his own nest without regard for the common good. Such a view would certainly not be true of individuals, though it would be more likely to apply in the case of closely associated interest groups, whose members are likely to support each other in their particular convictions. It is rather that when a number of rival theories and proposals for action offer themselves, the one to appeal most will be that which conforms most closely to one's experience and interest, particularly if one's associates are also vigorously in support. A suspicion that on strict internal logic, a rival but inconvenient theory might be preferable will then usually lead to its dismissal, in all honesty, on moral or other non-intellectual grounds. Still less will any interest group accept a theory, no matter how plausible at an abstract, intellectual level, which will directly harm its members. It will try to find an opposing theory if it possibly can, and if none is available it will still propose action to prevent damage to itself, even if it means denying theory altogether and operating by 'feel' or by 'moral sense' only. The application of economic theory in actual prac-

---

severe than those which have been the rule in recent years.' Quoted by Morgan-Webb, p. 61.

[1] See Essay 3 below.

[2] E.g. W. F. Crick, 'British Monetary Policy, 1931–37', *Bankers' Magazine*, CXLV (1938), p. 223.

tice is therefore a much more subtle process than Keynes was willing to credit. Thus it is inconceivable that the City (and the Treasury) would have supported the gold standard, and would have submitted to the consequent stagnation and unemployment, as well as the deadening 'Treasury view' on public works,[1] if it had directly suffered thereby – no matter what the current economic theory had to say on the topic. But as these policies were in its immediate interest, fitting in with the dream of a past golden age, allowing the belief in the moral superiority of the banking community, and saving the trouble of serious economic thought, they were vigorously supported by all the power which the City possessed, over the anguished protests of the rest of the community.

It is also not necessary to believe that Montagu Norman or his supporters were 'callous' about the plight of industry or the unemployed. To say that a man loves his own children is not to imply that he hates others; indeed, he might well love them, too, and risk his life getting them out of the way of city traffic. Yet the ordering of his business affairs does not become intelligible unless we remember that, in that connection, he thinks only of his own children. Similarly, it may well be that the Bank's Court and the Treasury were sensitive to the suffering in the country; indeed, we have noted that the Bank went out of its way to assist in industrial 'rationalization'.[2] But their chief direct concern was limited to that tiny section of the community which even its most fervent supporters credited with annual earnings of no more than £60–65 million, and for whose sake all the sacrifices were made.

It now becomes understandable why, after the débâcle of 1931, those responsible were so eager to blame their own in-

[1] It has been disputed that such a view existed. Keynes, questioning Hopkins of the Treasury, exclaimed in despair, 'It bends so much that I find difficulty in getting hold of it.' To which the skilled civil servant replied, 'Yes, I do not think that these views are capable of being put in the rigid form of a theoretical doctrine.' Macmillan Committee, *Evidence*, Q. 5625.

[2] According to Boyle, when Norman was asked by the Macmillan Committee for his reasons for starting the Bankers' Industrial Development Company, which was to finance rationalization schemes, the following dialogue ensued:

N.: 'Reasons, Mr Chairman? I don't have reasons, I have instincts.'

M.: 'We understand that, of course, Mr Governor, nevertheless you must have had *some* reasons.'

N.: 'Well, if I had I have forgotten them.' p. 327.

B

competence: they evidently thought that the more appropriate alternative – self-interest – was even more discreditable. Yet they were surely wrong. They could, with some justice, have turned the tables on their accusers and pointed out that it was society which had played a nasty trick on them. Brought up on the firm understanding that financial policy was concerned with British overseas credit, exchange rates and gold movements only; and following these time-honoured practices to the letter, they suddenly found themselves called upon to explain why their policy failed to take account of output and employment at home, which it had never before been suggested that it should. They had difficulty enough working a gold standard in which London was no longer the sole centre, but one of several, and in which no one country (least of all the United Kingdom) played the game according to the old 'rules'. They also had to adjust to a mechanism which, instead of reacting to internal fluctuations by placing the burden overseas, as the sterling gold standard had done before 1914, reacted to foreign fluctuations by placing the burden on home industry.[1] It was too much to expect them to be responsible for home industry as well, and to expose them to obloquy when they failed. They were quite unaware of having crossed the historical watershed between the *laissez-faire* society in which gold movements automatically settled the minor affair of the price level, and the modern economy, in which output and employment may be subject to conscious social control. When Sir Roy Harrod exclaims, 'Mr Norman closed all the doors. It did not seem to occur to him that, considering existing levels of unemployment, this amounted to a damning indictment of the system for which he was responsible',[2] he is exactly right. Such a thought had not occurred to Norman, and Churchill's moving appeals to the pundits in 1925[3] fell on totally deaf ears.

Thus the accusation of a 'banker's ramp', used with reference to the fall of the Labour Government, but never far from the surface in other discussions either, completely misses the mark. The fault lay with those who expected bankers to be patriotic, rather than looking after the interests of those who paid them;

[1] E.g. Reginald McKenna, *Post-War Banking Policy* (1928), pp. 16–17.
[2] Op. cit., pp. 419–20.
[3] Moggridge, pp. 45 ff.

yet no banking system could function for a day if bankers ever put patriotism first. The fact was that, apart from Norman himself, all the Directors of the Bank of England did have businesses of their own in which their main interest was bound to lie. They would not consciously favour their own pockets at the expense of the nation, but it was only human to assume that they would tend to believe that those policies were in the national interest which also happened to be in their own.

The most astonishing feature of this episode in British economic history was the survival of a Central Banking institution, enjoying full powers to affect in vital ways the economic health of society independently of the Government, yet itself representing a narrow section of the economy only and being responsible to no-one else. Here was a relic of bygone centuries, ages away even from the Northcote–Trevelyan reforms; a self-appointed corporation, recruiting its members neither by popular democratic election nor by ability and qualification, but by family descent and 'interest'. It owed no explanation to the electorate at large; it gave no information and refused to provide justifications for its doing. It enjoyed a monopolistic privilege, confirmed periodically by Parliament, without accounting for the errors it committed or the damage it did to others. It dominated the Treasury and, under Norman, even played at independent foreign politics. The forcing through of the Cunliffe financial policy which dominated Britain in 1920–31 was largely due to the power and 'expert' advice of the Bank of England, which in turn, depended and fed on the power of the City.

Yet there was little adverse reference to such an anomalous situation, except from the extreme left, before 1931. How was it that neither industry nor the Parliamentary Labour Party questioned the survival of this dangerous anachronism, even when they opposed its policies? The answer has to be sought in history. Most men still remembered the Bank in its glory before 1914, and attributed the golden age to the skill of the bankers rather than to its true source – the power of the British economy as a whole. At a deeper level, however, the British economy had entered that critical stage in the history of all industrial nations, as in that of most family dynasties, when the industrial power is overtaken by others but the creditor position remains. Britain appeared to be turning into a rentier economy, and the

City, in consequence, enjoyed an undeserved respect. Fortunately, the industrial power of Britain is by no means at an end; but the experience of the 1950s and 1960s is not designed to dispel the notion that among those making economic policies, the rentiers' or bankers' mentality with its emphasis on restriction and stagnation still holds sway.

1 The Economic Consequences of Mr Churchill[1]

J. M. KEYNES

[This abbreviated version was first published as chapter 5 of *Essays in Persuasion*, Macmillan, 1931.]

I THE MISLEADING OF MR CHURCHILL

The policy of improving the foreign-exchange value of sterling up to its pre-war value in gold from being about 10 per cent below it, means that, whenever we sell anything abroad, either the foreign buyer has to pay 10 per cent *more in his money* or we have to accept 10 per cent *less in our money*. That is to say, we have to reduce our sterling prices, for coal or iron or shipping freights or whatever it may be, by 10 per cent in order to be on a competitive level, unless prices rise elsewhere. Thus the policy of improving the exchange by 10 per cent involves a reduction of 10 per cent in the sterling receipts of our export industries.

Now, if these industries found that their expenses for wages and for transport and for rates and for everything else were falling 10 per cent at the same time, they could afford to cut their prices and would be no worse off than before. But, of course, this does not happen. Since they use, and their employees consume, all kinds of articles produced at home, it is impossible for them to cut their prices 10 per cent, unless wages and expenses in home industries generally have fallen 10 per cent. Meanwhile the weaker export industries are reduced to a bankrupt condition. Failing a fall in the value of gold itself, nothing can retrieve their position except a general fall of all internal prices and wages. Thus Mr Churchill's policy of improving the exchange by 10 per cent was, sooner or later, a policy of reducing every one's wages by 2*s*. in the £. He who wills the end wills the means. What now faces the Government is the ticklish

[1] [Written immediately after the Return to Gold.]

task of carrying out their own dangerous and unnecessary decision.

The movement away from eqilibrium began in October last (1924) and has proceeded, step by step, with the improvement of the exchange – brought about first by the anticipation, and then by the fact, of the restoration of gold, and not by an improvement in the intrinsic value of sterling.[1] The President of the Board of Trade has asserted in the House of Commons that the effect of the restoration of the gold standard upon our export trade has been 'all to the good'. The Chancellor of the Exchequer has expressed the opinion that the return to the gold standard is no more responsible for the condition of affairs in the coal industry than is the Gulf Stream. These statements are of the feather-brained order. It is open to Ministers to argue that the restoration of gold is worth the sacrifice and that the sacrifice is temporary. They can also say, with truth, that the industries which are feeling the wind most have private troubles of their own. When a *general* cause operates, those which are weak for other reasons are toppled over. But because an epidemic of influenza carries off only those who have weak hearts, it is not permissible to say that the influenza is 'all to the good', or that it has no more to do with the mortality than the Gulf Stream has.

The effect has been the more severe because we were not free from trouble a year ago. Whilst, at that date, sterling wages and sterling cost of living were in conformity with values in the United States, they were already too high compared with those in some European countries. It was also probable that certain of our export industries were overstocked both with plant and with labour, and that some transference of capital and of men into home industries was desirable and, in the long run, even inevitable. Thus we already had an awkward problem; and one of the arguments against raising the international value of sterling was the fact that it greatly aggravated, instead of mitigating, an existing disparity between

---

[1] This view was shared by the Treasury Committee on the Currency, who reported that the exchange improvement of last autumn and spring could not be maintained if we did not restore the gold standard; in other words, the improvement in the exchange prior to the restoration of gold was due to a speculative anticipation of this event and to a movement of capital, and not to an intrinsic improvement in sterling itself.

internal and external values, and that, by committing us to a period of Deflation, it necessarily postponed active measures of capital expansion at home, such as might facilitate the transference of labour into the home trades. British wages, measured in gold, are now 15 per cent higher than they were a year ago. The gold cost of living in England is now so high compared with what it is in Belgium, France, Italy and Germany that the workers in those countries can accept a gold wage 30 per cent lower than what our workers receive without suffering at all in the amount of their real wages. What wonder that our export trades are in trouble!

Our export industries are suffering because they are the *first* to be asked to accept the 10 per cent reduction. If *every one* was accepting a similar reduction at the same time, the cost of living would fall, so that the lower money wage would represent nearly the same real wage as before. But, in fact, there is no machinery for effecting a simultaneous reduction. Deliberately to raise the value of sterling money in England means, therefore, engaging in a struggle with each separate group in turn, with no prospect that the final result will be fair, and no guarantee that the stronger groups will not gain at the expense of the weaker.

The working classes cannot be expected to understand, better than Cabinet Ministers, what is happening. Those who are attacked first are faced with a depression of their standard of life, because the cost of living will not fall until all the others have been successfully attacked too; and, therefore, they are justified in defending themselves. Nor can the classes which are first subjected to a reduction of money wages be guaranteed that this will be compensated later by a corresponding fall in the cost of living, and will not accrue to the benefit of some other class. Therefore they are bound to resist so long as they can; and it must be war, until those who are economically weakest are beaten to the ground.

This state of affairs is not an inevitable consequence of a decreased capacity to produce wealth. I see no reason why, with good management, real wages need be reduced on the average. It is the consequence of a misguided monetary policy.

These arguments are not arguments against the gold standard as such. That is a separate discussion which I shall not touch here. They are arguments against having restored gold in conditions which required a substantial readjustment of all our money values. If Mr Churchill had restored gold by fixing the parity lower than the pre-war figure, or if he had waited until our money values were adjusted to the pre-war parity, then these particular arguments would have no force. But in doing what he did in the actual circumstances of last spring, he was just asking for trouble. For he was committing himself to force down money wages and all money values, without any idea how it was to be done. Why did he do such a silly thing?

Partly, perhaps, because he has no instinctive judgement to prevent him from making mistakes; partly because, lacking this instinctive judgement, he was deafened by the clamorous voices of conventional finance; and, most of all, because he was gravely misled by his experts.

His experts made, I think, two serious mistakes. In the first place, I suspect that they miscalculated the degree of the maladjustment of money values which would result from restoring sterling to its pre-war gold parity, because they attended to index numbers of prices which were irrelevant or inappropriate to the matter in hand. If you want to know whether sterling values are adjusting themselves to an improvement in the exchange, it is useless to consider, for example, the price of raw cotton in Liverpool. This *must* adjust itself to a movement of the exchange, because, in the case of an imported raw material, the parity of international values is necessarily maintained almost hour by hour. But it is not sensible to argue from this that the money wages of dockers or of charwomen and the cost of postage or of travelling by train also adjust themselves hour by hour in accordance with the foreign exchanges. Yet this, I fancy, is what the Treasury did. They compared the usual wholesale index numbers here and in America, and – since these are made up to the extent of at least two-thirds from the raw materials of international commerce, the prices of which necessarily adjust themselves to the exchanges – the true disparity of internal prices was watered down to a fraction of its true value. This led them to think that the gap to be bridged was perhaps 2 or 3 per cent, instead of the true figure of 10 or 12 per cent, which was the indication given by the index numbers of the cost of living, of the level of wages, and of the prices of our manufactured exports – which indexes are a much better rough-and-ready guide for this purpose, particularly if they agree with one another, than are the index numbers of wholesale prices.

But I think that Mr Churchill's experts also misunderstood and underrated the technical difficulty of bringing about a general reduction of internal money values. When we raise the value of sterling by 10 per cent we transfer about £1,000 million into the pockets of the rentiers out of the pockets of the rest of us, and we increase the real burden of the National Debt by some £750 million (thus wiping out the benefit of all our laborious contributions to the Sinking Fund since the war). This, which is bad enough, is inevitable. But there would be no other bad consequences if only there was some way of bringing about a simultaneous reduction of 10 per cent in all other money payments; when the process was complete we should each of us have nearly the same real income as before. I think that the minds of his advisers still dwelt in the imaginary academic world, peopled by City editors, members of Cunliffe and Currency Committees *et hoc genus omne*, where the necessary adjustments follow 'automatically' from a 'sound' policy by the Bank of England.

The theory is that depression in the export industries, which are admittedly hit first, coupled if necessary with dear money and credit restriction, *diffuse* themselves evenly and fairly rapidly throughout the whole community. But the professors of this theory do not tell us in plain language how the diffusion takes place.

Mr Churchill asked the Treasury Committee on the Currency to advise him on these matters. He declared in his Budget speech that their report 'contains a reasoned marshalling of the arguments which have convinced His Majesty's Government.' Their arguments – if their vague and jejune meditations can be called such – are there for anyone to read. What they ought to have said, but did not say, can be expressed as follows:

Money wages, the cost of living, and the prices which we are asking for our exports have not adjusted themselves to the improvement in the exchange, which the expectation of your restoring the gold standard, in accordance with your repeated declarations, has already brought about. They are about 10 per cent too high. If, therefore, you fix the exchange at this gold parity, you must either gamble on a rise in gold prices abroad, which will induce foreigners to pay a higher gold price for our exports, or you are committing yourself to a policy of forcing down money wages and the cost of living to the necessary extent.

We must warn you that this latter policy is not easy. It is certain to involve unemployment and industrial disputes. If, as some people think, real wages were already too high a year ago, that is all the worse, because the amount of the necessary wage reductions in terms of money will be all the greater.

The gamble on a rise in gold prices abroad may quite likely succeed. But it is by no means certain, and you must be prepared for the other contingency. If you think that the advantages of the gold standard are so significant and so urgent that you are prepared to risk great unpopularity and to take stern administrative action in order to secure them, the course of events will probably be as follows:

To begin with, there will be great depression in the export industries. This in itself will be helpful, since it will produce an atmosphere favourable to the reduction of wages. The cost of living will fall somewhat. This will be helpful too, because it will give you a good argument in favour of reducing wages. Nevertheless, the cost of living will not fall sufficiently, and, consequently, the export industries will not be able to reduce their prices sufficiently until wages have fallen in the sheltered industries. Now wages will not fall in the sheltered industries merely because there is unemployment in the unsheltered industries, therefore you will have to see to it that there is unemployment in the sheltered industries also. The way to do this will be by credit restriction. By means of the restriction of credit by the Bank of England you can deliberately intensify unemployment to any required degree until wages *do* fall. When the process is complete the cost of living will have fallen too, and we shall then be, with luck, just where we were before we started.

We ought to warn you, though perhaps this is going a little outside our proper sphere, that it will not be safe politically to admit that you are intensifying unemployment deliberately in order to reduce wages. Thus you will have to ascribe what is happening to every conceivable cause except the true one. We estimate that about two years may elapse before it will be safe for you to utter in public one single word of truth. By that time you will either be out of office or the adjustment, somehow or other, will have been carried through.

II THE BALANCE OF TRADE AND THE BANK OF ENGLAND

The effect of a high exchange is to diminish the sterling prices both of imports and of exports. The result is both to encourage imports and to discourage exports, thus turning the balance of trade against us. It is at this stage that the Bank of England becomes interested; for if nothing was done we should have to pay the adverse balance in gold. The Bank of England has applied, accordingly, two effective remedies. The first remedy is to put obstacles in the way of our usual lending abroad by means of an embargo on foreign loans and, recently, on colonial loans also; and the second remedy is to encourage the United States to lend us money by maintaining the unprecedented situation of a bill rate one per cent higher in London than in New York.

The efficacy of these two methods for balancing our account is beyond doubt – I believe that they might remain efficacious for a considerable length of time. For we start with a wide margin of strength. Before the war our capacity to lend abroad was, according to the Board of Trade, about £181 million, equivalent to £280 million at the present price level; and even in 1923 the Board of Trade estimated our net surplus at £102 million. Since new foreign investments bring in no immediate return, it follows that we can reduce our exports by £100 million a year, without any risk of insolvency, provided we reduce our foreign investments by the same amount. So far as the maintenance of the gold standard is concerned, it is a matter of indifference whether we have £100 million worth of foreign investment or £100 million worth of unemployment. If those who used to produce exports lose their job, nevertheless, our financial equilibrium remains perfect, and the Governor of the Bank of England runs no risk of losing gold, provided that the loans, which were formerly paid over in the shape of those exports, are curtailed to an equal extent. Moreover, our credit as a borrower is still very good. By paying a sufficiently high rate of interest, we can not only meet any deficit but the Governor can borrow, in addition, whatever quantity of gold it may amuse him to publish in his weekly return.

The President of the Board of Trade calculates that, during the year ended last May, it is probable that there was no actual deficit on our trade account, which was about square. If this is correct, there must be a substantial deficit now. In addition, the embargo on foreign investment is only partially successful. It cannot hold back all types of foreign issues and it cannot prevent British investors from purchasing securities direct from New York. It is here, therefore, that the Bank of England's other remedy comes in. By maintaining discount rates in London at a sufficient margin above discount rates in New York, it can induce the New York money market to lend a sufficient sum to the London money market to balance both our trade deficit and the foreign investments which British investors are still buying in spite of the embargo. Besides, when once we have offered high rates of interest to attract funds from the New York short-loan market, we have to continue them, even though we have no need to increase our borrowings, in order to retain what we have already borrowed.

Nevertheless, the policy of maintaining money rates in London at a level which will attract and retain loans from New York does not really differ in any important respect from the French policy, which we have so much condemned, of supporting the exchange with the help of loans from Messrs J. P. Morgan. Our policy would only differ from the French policy if the high rate of discount was not only intended to attract American money, but was also part of a policy for restricting credit at home. This is the aspect to which we must now attend.

To pay for unemployment by changing over from being a lending country to being a borrowing country is admittedly a disastrous course, and I do not doubt that the authorities of the Bank of England share this view. They dislike the embargo on foreign issues, and they dislike having to attract short-loan money from New York. They may do these things to gain a breathing space; but, if they are to live up to their own principles, they must use the breathing space to effect what are euphemistically called 'the fundamental adjustments'. With this object in view there is only one step which lies within their power – namely, to restrict credit. This, in the circumstances, is the orthodox policy of the gold party; the adverse trade balance indicates that our prices are too high, and the way to bring them down is by dear money and the restriction of credit. When this medicine has done its work, there will no longer be any need to restrict foreign loans or to borrow abroad.

Now what does this mean in plain language? Our problem is to reduce money wages and, through them, the cost of living, with the idea that, when the circle is complete, real wages will be as high, or nearly as high, as before. By what *modus operandi* does credit restriction attain this result?

In no other way than by the deliberate intensification of unemployment. The object of credit restriction, in such a case, is to withdraw from employers the financial means to employ labour at the existing level of prices and wages. The policy can only attain its end by intensifying unemployment without limit, until the workers are ready to accept the necessary reduction of money wages under the pressure of hard facts.

This is the so-called 'sound' policy, which is demanded as a result of the rash act of pegging sterling at a gold value, which it did not – measured in its purchasing power over British labour – possess as yet. It is a policy, nevertheless, from which any humane or judicious person must shrink. So far as I can judge, the Governor of the Bank of England shrinks from it. But what is he to do, swimming, with his boat burnt, between the devil and the deep sea? At present, it appears, he compromises. He applies the 'sound' policy half-heartedly; he avoids calling things by their right names; and he hopes – this is his best chance – that something will turn up.

The Bank of England works with so much secrecy and so much concealment of important statistics that it is never easy to state with precision what it is doing. The credit restriction already in force has been effected in several ways which are partly independent. First, there is the embargo on new issues which probably retards the normal rate of the circulation of money; then in March the bank rate was raised; more recently market rate was worked up nearer to bank rate; lastly – and far the most important of all – the Bank has manoeuvred its assets and liabilities in such a way as to reduce the amount of cash available to the Clearing Banks as a basis for credit. This last is the essential instrument of credit restriction. Failing direct information, the best reflection of the amount of this restriction is to be found in the deposits of the Clearing Banks. The tendency of these to fall indicates some significant degree of restriction. Owing, however, to seasonal fluctuations and to the artificial character of the end-June returns, it is not yet possible to estimate with accuracy how much restriction has taken place in the last three months. So far as one can judge, the amount of direct restriction is not yet considerable. But no one can say how much more restriction may become necessary if we continue on our present lines.

Nevertheless, even these limited measures are responsible, in my opinion, for an important part of the recent intensification of unemployment. Credit restriction is an incredibly powerful instrument, and even a little of it goes a long way – especially in circumstances where the opposite course is called for. The policy of deliberately intensifying unemployment with a view to forcing wage reductions is already partly in force, and the tragedy of our situation lies in the fact that, from the misguided standpoint which has been officially adopted, this course is theoretically justifiable. No section of labour will readily accept lower wages merely in response to sentimental speeches, however genuine, by Mr Baldwin. We are depending for the reduction of wages on the pressure of unemployment and of strikes and lock-outs; and in order to make sure of this result we are deliberately intensifying the unemployment.

The Bank of England is *compelled* to curtail credit by all the rules of the gold standard game. It is acting conscientiously and 'soundly' in doing so. But this does not alter the fact that to keep a tight hold on credit – and no one will deny that the Bank is doing that – necessarily involves intensifying unemployment in the present circumstances of this country. What we need to restore prosperity today is an easy credit policy. We want to encourage business men to enter on new enterprises, not, as we are doing, to discourage them. Deflation does not reduce wages 'automatically'. It reduces them by causing unemployment. The proper object of dear money is to check an incipient boom. Woe to those whose faith leads them to use it to aggravate a depression!

I should pick out coal as being above all others a victim of our monetary policy. On the other hand, it is certainly true that the reason why the coal industry presents so dismal a picture to the eye is because it has other troubles which have weakened its power of resistance and have left it no margin of strength with which to support a new misfortune.

In these circumstances the colliery owners propose that the gap should be bridged by a reduction of wages, irrespective of a reduction in the cost of living – that is to say, by a lowering in the standard of life of the miners. They are to make this sacrifice to meet circumstances for which they are in no way responsible and over which they have no control.

It is a grave criticism of our way of managing our economic affairs that this should seem to any one to be a reasonable proposal; though it is equally unreasonable that the colliery owner should suffer the loss, except on the principle that it is the capitalist who bears the risk. If miners were free to transfer themselves to other industries, if a collier out of work or underpaid could offer himself as a baker, a bricklayer or a railway porter at a lower wage than is now current in these industries, it would be another matter. But notoriously they are not so free. Like other victims of economic transition in past times, the miners are to be offered the choice between starvation and submission, the fruits of their submission to accrue to the benefit of other classes. But in view of the disappearance of an effective mobility of labour and of a competitive wage level between different industries, I am not sure that they are not worse placed in some ways than their grandfathers were.

Why should coal miners suffer a lower standard of life than other classes of labour? They may be lazy, good-for-nothing fellows who do not work so hard or so long as they should. But is there any evidence that they are more lazy or more good-for-nothing than other people?

On grounds of social justice, no case can be made out for reducing the wages of the miners. They are the victims of the economic Juggernaut. They represent in the flesh the 'fundamental adjustments' engineered by the Treasury and the Bank of England to satisfy the impatience of the City fathers to bridge the 'moderate gap' between $4·40 and $4·86. *They* (and others to follow) are the 'moderate sacrifice' still necessary to ensure the stability of the gold standard. The plight of the coal miners is the first, but not – unless we are very lucky – the last, of the Economic Consequences of Mr Churchill.

The truth is that we stand mid-way between two theories of economic society. The one theory maintains that wages should be fixed by reference to what is 'fair' and 'reasonable' as between classes. The other theory – the theory of the economic Juggernaut – is that wages should be settled by economic pressure, otherwise called 'hard facts', and that our vast machine should crash along, with regard only to its equilibrium as a whole, and without attention to the chance consequences of the journey to individual groups.

The gold standard, with its dependence on pure chance, its faith in 'automatic adjustments', and its general regardlessness of social detail, is an essential emblem and idol of those who sit in the top tier of the machine. I think that they are immensely rash in their regardlessness, in their vague optimism and comfortable belief that nothing really serious ever happens. Nine times out of ten, nothing really serious does happen – merely a little distress to individuals or to groups. But we run a risk of the tenth time (and are stupid into the bargain) if we continue to apply the principles of an economics which was worked out on the hypotheses of *laissez-faire* and free competition to a society which is rapidly abandoning these hypotheses.

III IS THERE A REMEDY?

The monetary policy announced in the Budget (of 1925) being the real source of our industrial troubles, it is impossible to recommend any truly satisfactory course except its reversal. Nevertheless, amongst the alternatives still open to this Government, some courses are better than others.

One course is to pursue the so-called 'sound' policy vigorously, with the object of bringing about 'the fundamental adjustments' in the orthodox way by further restricting credit and raising the bank rate in the autumn if necessary, thus intensifying unemployment and using every other weapon in our hands to force down money wages, trusting in the belief that, when the process is finally complete, the cost of living will have fallen also, thus restoring average real wages to their former level. If this policy can be carried through it will be, in a sense, successful, though it will leave much injustice behind it on account of the inequality of the changes it will effect, the stronger groups gaining at the expense of the weaker. For the method of economic pressure, since it bears most hardly on the weaker industries, where wages are already relatively low, tends to increase the existing disparities between the wages of different industrial groups.

The question is how far public opinion will allow such a policy to go. It would be politically impossible for the Government to admit that it was deliberately intensifying unemployment, even though the members of the Currency Committee were to supply them with an argument for it. On the other hand, it is possible for Deflation to produce its effects without being recognized. Deflation, once started ever so little, is cumulative in its progress. If pessimism becomes generally prevalent in the business world, the slower circulation of money resulting from this can carry Deflation a long way further, without the Bank having either to raise the bank rate or to reduce its deposits. And since the public always understands particular causes better than general causes, the depression which will be attributed to the industrial disputes which will accompany it, to the Dawes Scheme, to China, to the inevitable consequences of the Great War, to tariffs, to high taxation, to anything in the world except the general monetary policy which has set the whole thing going.

Moreover, this course need not be pursued in a clear-cut way. A furtive restriction of credit by the Bank of England can be coupled with vague cogitations on the part of Mr Baldwin (who has succeeded to the position in our affections formerly occupied by Queen Victoria) as to whether social benevolence does not require him to neutralize the effects of this by a series of illogical subsidies. Queen Baldwin's good heart will enable us to keep our tempers, whilst the serious work goes on behind the scenes. The Budgetary position will render it impossible for the subsidies to be big enough to make any real difference. And in the end, unless there is a social upheaval, the 'fundamental adjustments' will duly take place.

Some people may contemplate this forecast with equanimity. I do not. It involves a great loss of social income whilst it is going on, and will leave behind much social injustice when it is finished. The best, indeed the only, hope lies in the possibility that in this world, where so little can be foreseen, something may turn up – which leads me to my alternative suggestions. Could we not *help* something to turn up?

There are just two features of the situation which are capable of being turned to our advantage. The first is financial – if the value of gold would fall in the outside world, that would render unnecessary any important change in the level of wages here. The second is industrial – if the cost of living would fall *first*, our consciences would be clear in asking Labour to accept a lower money wage, since it would then be evident that the reduction was not part of a plot to reduce real wages.

When the return to the gold standard was first announced, many authorities agreed that we were gambling on rising prices in the United States. The rise has not taken place, so far.[1] Moreover, the policy of the Bank of England has been calculated to steady prices in the United States rather than to raise them. The fact that American banks can lend their funds in London at a high rate of interest tends to keep money rates in New York higher than they would be otherwise, and to draw to London, instead of to New York, the oddments of surplus gold in the world markets. Thus our policy has been to relieve New York of the pressure of cheap money and additional gold which would tend otherwise to force their prices upwards. The abnormal difference between money rates in London and New York is preventing the gold standard from working even according to its own principles. According to orthodox doctrine, when prices are too high in A as compared with B, gold flows out from A and into B, thus lowering prices in A and *raising them in B*, so that an upward movement in B's prices meets half-way the downward movement in A's.

At present the policy of the Bank of England prevents this

---

[1] In my opinion, we need not yet abandon the hope that it will take place. The tendency of American prices is upwards, rather than downwards, and it only requires a match to set alight the dormant possibilities of inflation in the United States. This possibility is the one real ground for not being too pessimistic.

from happening. I suggest, therefore, that they should reverse this policy. Let them reduce the bank rate, and cease to restrict credit. If, as a result of this, the 'bad' American money, which is now a menace to the London money market, begins to flow back again, let us pay it off in gold or, if necessary, by using the dollar credits which the Treasury and the Bank of England have arranged in New York. It would be better to pay in gold, because it would be cheaper and because the flow of actual gold would have more effect on the American price level. If we modified the rules which now render useless three-quarters of our stock of gold, we could see with equanimity a loss of £60 million or £70 million in gold – which would make a great difference to conditions elsewhere. There is no object in paying 4½ per cent interest on floating American balances which can leave us at any moment, in order to use these balances to buy and hold idle and immobilized gold.

Gold could not flow out on this scale, unless at the same time the Bank of England was abandoning the restriction of credit and was replacing the gold by some other asset, e.g. Treasury Bills. That is to say, the Bank would have to abandon the attempt to bring about the fundamental adjustments by the methods of economic pressure and the deliberate intensification of unemployment. Therefore, taken by itself, this policy might be open to the criticism that it was staking too much on the expectation of higher prices in America.

To meet this, I suggest that Mr Baldwin should face the facts frankly and sincerely, in collaboration with the trade union leaders, on the following lines.

So long as members of the Cabinet continue to pretend that the present movement to reduce wages has nothing to do with the value of money, it is natural that the working classes should take it as a concerted attack on real wages. If the Chancellor of the Exchequer is right in his view that his monetary policy has had no more to do with the case than the Gulf Stream, then it follows that the present agitations to lower wages are simply a campaign against the standard of life of the working classes. It is only when the Government have admitted the truth of the diagnosis set forth in these chapters that they are in a position to invite the collaboration of the trade union leaders on fair and reasonable terms.

As soon as the Government admit that the problem is primarily a monetary one, then they can say to Labour

> This is not an attack on real wages. We have raised the value of sterling 10 per cent. This means that money wages must fall 10 per cent. But it also means, when the adjustment is complete, that the cost of living will fall about 10 per cent. In this case there will have been no serious fall in real wages. Now there are two alternative ways of bringing about the reduction of money wages. One way is to apply economic pressure and to intensify unemployment by credit restriction until wages are *forced down*. This is a hateful and disastrous way, because of its unequal effects on the stronger and on the weaker groups, and because of the economic and social waste whilst it is in progress. The other way is to effect a *uniform* reduction of wages by *agreement*, on the understanding that this shall not mean in the long run any fall in average real wages below what they were in the first quarter of this year. The practical difficulty is that money wages and the cost of living are interlocked. The cost of living cannot fall until *after* money wages have fallen. Money wages must fall *first* in order to allow the cost of living to fall. Can we not agree, therefore, to have a uniform initial reduction of money wages throughout the whole range of employment, including Government and Municipal employment, of (say) 5 per cent, which reduction shall not hold good unless, after an interval, it has been compensated by a fall in the cost of living?

If Mr Baldwin were to make this proposal the trade union leaders would probably ask him at once what he intended to do about money payments other than wages – rents, profits, and interest. As regards rents and profits, he can reply that these are not fixed in terms of money, and will therefore fall, when measured in money, step by step with prices. The worst of this reply is that rents and profits, like wages, are sticky and may not fall quick enough to help the transition as much as they should. As regards the interest on bonds, however, and particularly the interest on the National Debt, he has no answer at all. For it is of the essence of any policy to lower prices that it benefits the receivers of interest at the expense of the rest of the community; this consequence of deflation is deeply embedded in our system of money contract. On the whole, I do not see how Labour's objection can be met, except by the rough-and-ready expedient of levying an additional income-tax of 1*s.* in the £ on all income other than from employments, which should continue until real wages had recovered to their previous level.[1]

If the proposal to effect a voluntary all-round reduction of wages, whilst sound in principle, is felt to be too difficult to achieve in practice, then, for my part, I should be inclined to stake everything on an attempt to raise prices in the outside world – that is on a reversal of the present policy of the Bank of England. This, I understand from their July *Monthly Review*, is also the recommendation of the high authorities of the Midland Bank.

That there should be grave difficulties in all these suggestions is inevitable. Any plan, such as the Government has adopted, for deliberately altering the value of money, must, in modern economic conditions, come up against objections of justice and expediency. They are suggestions to mitigate the harsh consequences of a mistake; but they cannot undo the mistake. They will not commend themselves to those pessimists who believe that it is the level of real wages, and not merely of money wages, which is the proper object of attack. I mention them because our present policy of deliberately intensifying unemployment by keeping a tight hold on credit, just when on other grounds it ought to be relaxed, so as to force adjustments by using the weapon of economic necessity against individuals and against particular industries, is a policy which the country would never permit if it knew what was being done.

---

[1] This will not prevent bondholders from gaining in the long run, if in the long run prices do not rise again. But such profits and losses to bondholders are an inevitable feature of an unstable monetary standard. Since, however, prices generally do rise in the long run, bondholders in the long run are losers, not gainers, from the system.

2 The Conflict of Opinion and Economic Interest in England

W. ADAMS BROWN, Jr

[First published as chapter 10 of *England and the New Gold Standard, 1919–1926*, Yale University Press, New Haven, 1929.]

The final efforts put forth by England during 1924 and 1925 in restoring the old parity and maintaining it when restored, brought in their train a discussion of the principles and problems involved which is in itself an interesting subject of investigation. In the main the opinions expressed, in so far as they were contradictory, reflected a cleavage of economic interest between different sections of the community. It is not the purpose of this study to record opinions, but to chronicle and attempt to interpret facts, and the brief account given in this chapter of the position taken by various participants in the gold standard debate will be designed to illustrate this cleavage of interest, and to set in relief the economic antagonisms which the policy actually pursued in the return to gold inevitably aroused. This will necessarily mean directing attention in some measure away from the more spectacular aspects of the debate, which were the result of a fundamental difference of view between the supporters of the gold standard on the one hand and Mr Maynard Keynes on the other as to the type of monetary standard best suited to serve the future interest of British economic life. These important discussions of underlying monetary theory, however, quite aside from their intrinsic interest, helped to throw light upon the temper in which England approached the return to gold, and cannot be passed over entirely in an historical treatment of this subject.

The official case for the return to the gold standard at the time and in the manner actually chosen is contained in the first instance in the Report of the Committee on the Currency and Bank of England Note Issues. The arguments presented by the Committee were brief and clear as far as they went.[1] They did not deal at all with the question of the general desirability of a gold standard from the point of view of the interests of the different social classes affected by its operation. The general advantages of a gold standard were not stated by the Report, but were rather taken for granted as self-evident (e.g. Sec. 16). One particular advantage of such a standard was, however, stressed. By a drain of gold, the Report held, the gold standard gives a sure indication of the existence of national over-lending, and further it provides an automatic stop to it (Sec. 34). The advantages offered by alternative plans were summarily disposed of. Devaluation was rejected without argument as having at all times been unworthy of consideration[2] (Secs. 6 and 7). In the main the Report considered only questions of when, and how (Sec. 9). The question 'When?' was dealt with by a threefold argument. In the first place it was declared that the ability to return to gold at once did in fact exist, because

> our existing volume of exports, visible and invisible, together with the income we derive from foreign investments, is still undoubtedly sufficient to meet our foreign debts and pay for our necessary imports and even to supply a moderate balance for new foreign investment. [Sec. 12].

In the second place an argument of expediency was used, based upon the *fait accompli* of the over-valuation of the pound (Secs. 18, 19 and 20). A serious obstacle to the return to gold was recognized as existing in the discrepancy between the English and the American price levels, estimated in the Report itself at about 10 per cent. The maintenance of a free gold market was conceived of as depending upon an adjustment between the two, and the old problem of whether to have further deflation in England or wait for inflation in America was again envisaged (Sec. 16). The Report solved this problem by an argument, the essence of which is found in Section 20, and which runs in part as follows:

---

[1] The adjective chosen by Mr Keynes to describe them, however, was 'jejune', and this was not without some degree of justification.

[2] Underlying this summary rejection of devaluation there was undoubtedly the strong feeling held in many very influential quarters in England that the return to the old gold parity involved a moral issue, a question of obligation and honour This feeling is well expressed by a phrase used by Sir Henry Strakosch in the course of a later controversy with Mr Keynes, in which he referred to 'devaluation – more appropriately called repudiation.' Letter to *The Times*, 31 July, 1925.

The adjustment of price levels required to restore and maintain pre-war parity needs to be only some $1\frac{1}{2}$ per cent larger than that required to hold the exchange at its present rate. If the adjustment of price levels necessary to attain this end is long deferred the exchange will inevitably fall back to the rate justified by comparative price levels or below it, since the psychological causes which have operated to force it up will tend to act in the other direction – and a period of fluctuating values is likely to ensue. To allow the exchange to fall back now, with the certainty of having later on to raise it again, would be a short-sighted policy injurious to trade and industry. But if this view is accepted and we are prepared to face any price adjustment which may be necessary to maintain the present exchange rate, there is nothing to be said for refusing to accept the very small ($1\frac{1}{2}$ per cent) extra adjustment involved in the re-establishment of an effective gold standard.[1]

Finally the pressure from the Dominions and the probable return to gold by other countries was pointed out as indicating the need for quick action. On the basis of these considerations, the question 'When?' was answered, 'Now'.

The answer to the question 'How?' was contained in a series of recommendations calling for action both by the Government and by the Bank of England. The former were put into effect following the Budget speech of the Chancellor of the Exchequer, and, with one exception, have been described at the close of the last chapter. That was the recommendation that the Cunliffe limit on the Treasury note issue be strictly maintained. This recommendation was clearly deflationary in character and was reinforced by two suggestions concerning Bank of

[1] The strongest point in this argument of the Committee is the emphasis laid upon the possible ill effects of loss of confidence which might have resulted from failure to return to gold. The argument assumes that it would have been injurious to British trade and industry to allow the sterling–dollar rate to fall to the true purchasing power parity between England and America, and then to raise it to the Mint parity at a later time. But whether or not such a policy would have had these injurious results would have depended upon the course of British and American prices in the interval. If it was to be the British policy to *force* the exchange rate to the old parity in any event in a short time even if this involved again overvaluing the pound and causing deflation in England, the whole argument is reduced to one between immediate and deferred action. It treats the real issue as already decided.

England policy. The first of these was that money rates should be raised if necessary to protect the gold standard (Sec. 32), and the second was that in case of need the gold reserves of the Bank of England should be liberally used, and that, if the foreign credits were drawn upon, the amounts withdrawn should be treated 'from the point of view of the Bank of England's monetary policy as equivalent to a corresponding loss from its own reserves', (Sec. 30).

Upon these arguments and suggestions the British Government acted. The speech of Mr Winston Churchill in presenting his Budget on 28 April, 1925,[1] which incorporated the practical recommendations of the Report, did not greatly increase the number and weight of the arguments advanced, though it undoubtedly added to the eloquence of their expression. Mr Churchill, however, did stress the continuity of British policy in connection with the return to gold in the following words:

> A return to the gold standard has long been a settled and declared policy of this country. Every Expert Conference since the war . . . has urged in principle the return to the gold standard. No responsible authority has advocated any other policy.

He also stressed the importance of the simultaneous action of Holland, the Dutch East Indies, Australia and New Zealand, and the proposed return of South Africa, as well as the previous adoption of the gold standard by other countries. The advantages of this common international action were pictured by Mr Churchill in a metaphor, which came very close to admitting the main contentions of Mr Keynes, and which ran as follows:

> That standard (the gold standard) may of course vary in itself from time to time, but the position of all countries related to it will vary together like ships in a harbour whose gangways are joined and who rise and fall together with the tide.[2]

---

[1] 183 *H.C. Deb.* 5*s.*, pp. 52–7.

[2] Mr Churchill speaks of ships riding in a *harbour*, but the realities of the case would have been more truly brought out had he pictured them loosely bound together in an open roadstead, rising and falling with the tide, it is true, but grinding and crashing against each other in the waves. This would have brought out not only the general rise and fall of price levels in all gold standard countries, but their constant readjustment to each other.

The Report of the Committee on the Currency and Bank of England Note Issues has been stressed not because it was the best presentation of the case for the gold standard. It did not meet the arguments advanced by Mr Keynes against that standard. It was not nearly as searching a discussion of the economic issues involved as may be found in many other sources.[1] It has been stressed because, by virtue of the action based upon it, it has become a fact of British history. As such it requires a more prominent place in an historical study of the return to gold than would or ought to be assigned to it in a discussion devoted to the development of monetary theory during this period.

The argument of the Committee based on the *fait accompli* of sterling-overvaluation was a curious one. It was, in fact, a statement that the adjustment of the rate of exchange to a point where it would reflect the purchasing power parity, followed by subsequent increase in the rate would be injurious to trade. Not the adjustment in price levels involved, but the fluctuation in the exchange was held to be the undesirable element in such a policy. This argument presents, although it does not explicitly state, one of the fundamental issues stressed by Mr Keynes, namely, the question as to whether it is wiser to adjust price levels to a fixed exchange rate, or to adjust the exchange rate to a fixed price level. It is important to note that the point of departure of both the supporters of the gold standard and of Mr Keynes was the same, namely, that the exchange rate must roughly represent the purchasing power parity. Mr Keynes held that it was more logical and more consistent with social justice that when an adjustment in the exchange rate or the price level, including wages, had to be made to bring this relationship about, this adjustment should be in the rate of exchange, and not in the price level. If there were a choice between a stable price level and a stable exchange, Mr Keynes was in favour of sacrificing the stable exchange.[2] Under the rules of 'the gold standard game', however, the

[1] In the writings of Prof. T. E. Gregory and Prof. Cannan, for example, or in the answers of Sir John Bradbury to Mr Keynes or in the speeches of Mr A. W. Kiddy.

[2] For example, in a letter to *The Times* on 1 August, 1925, Mr Keynes says in the course of an argument with Sir H. Strakosch, 'I would deliberately utilize fluctuations in the exchange as the shock absorber.'

choice must be the opposite one. Stable prices must yield to a stable exchange, and the advantages thus gained, he held, were not commensurate with the costs involved. If the great sacrifices made by England in the reconstruction period were to bear a fruit commensurate with their size, it must be a monetary system which would at least eliminate the continued fluctuations in the price level which were imposed by the very principles of gold standard technique.[1] Such a system was the managed currency championed by Mr Keynes.[2]

No attempt will be made to do justice to the full weight of the position represented by Mr Keynes and his followers. As a

[1] It was at this point that Mr Keynes was most universally misunderstood, particularly by the embattled City Editors of the London papers, with whom he carried on a conflict in the financial columns throughout a large part of 1925. When the relative instability of prices under inconvertible paper compared to their stability under gold was continually presented as the *coup de grâce* destroying his position, he was driven to retort in a letter to the City Editor of the *Morning Post* on 1 August, 1925, in the following terms:

I must also state what your City Editor must surely know well, that to assert that the management of the currency in the country prior to the readoption of gold had my approval, is a gross travesty of my opinions. I criticized it repeatedly and vehemently.

It is typical of the silliness and utter lack of intellectual standards by which this controversy is carried on by City Editors that because I am in favour of managing the currency *with a view to stability of prices*, I am therefore supposed to be in favour of managing it *with a view to instability of prices*. Sometimes I am said to have favoured deflation, as in your columns, and sometimes of inflation as in the columns of your contemporaries.

[2] J. M. Keynes, *A Tract on Monetary Reform*, (London, 1924) *passim*.

J. M. Keynes, Letter to *The Times*, 4 September, 1925, p. 20.

A concise summary of the position taken by the Cambridge School is given in the testimony of Mr Keynes before the Commercial Committee of Parliament on 4 March, 1925, after the cause was lost. This testimony was in effect as follows: The real distinction between the orthodox and the reforming party is one of *object*. The main object of the gold standard is to establish a uniform standard of currency which should be the same over a great part of the world, and which shall be independent of national politics. This demands regulation of the British credit system with reference not solely or even mainly to British internal requirements, but to the conditions of credit in the world at large, and more particularly in the United States. The main object of the monetary reformers is to evolve a standard of currency regulated primarily by the requirements of the credit system at home and of stability of internal prices even when this is only possible at the expense of fluctuations in terms of the standards of other countries. The methods of currency management are almost exactly the same under both standards. Under the gold standard the object will be to keep the percentage of gold in reserve within a certain number of points above or below a normal figure. Under the Stable Purchasing Power Standard the object would be to keep (say) the Board of Trade Index Number within a certain number of points above or below a normal figure. – *Bankers' Magazine*, (London, April 1925).

matter of history their views were overborne. As a matter of economic theory and as offering a future alternative to the gold standard when that standard shall have outlived its usefulness, they are worthy of the careful and extended study which has been given to them by economic students. It is a point of view that needed to be presented and deserved the brilliant championship it received. But within the boundaries marked out for this study it must be treated only so far as it throws light on the cleavage of economic interest involved in the actual return to gold.

Throughout 1924, as the rise in the value of the pound proceeded to gain more and more impetus under the influences which have been described, the question as to the desirability of an early return to gold came more and more to the fore in English discussion. The advocates of an early return, of delay, and of the managed currency became more and more vocal. But few clear expressions of opinion came from industry itself, the effects of the proposed return to gold upon which were being so actively debated. The general tone of industrial opinion was agnostic towards the question of the return to gold. This was due partly to the great prestige enjoyed by banking interests in England. Industrialists were, in general, content to allow questions of monetary policy to be discussed and decided by the bankers, as competent and expert in these matters. In part it was due to the fact that fluctuations in the exchange were felt to be only one, and in fact a minor one, among the many complex elements which entered into the determination of export prices and the demand for British goods abroad. Moreover, it was an element the influence of which upon export prices could not be determined with any precision. The rise of sterling towards parity did not, in fact, present itself *as a separate problem* to British industry in general and to the export industries in particular. It was only very gradually that the loss of orders in the export trades which became greater and greater as 1924 progressed came to be associated with the increasing value of the pound sterling in the foreign exchanges. Attention had almost exclusively been fixed upon the competition met with from countries with depreciating currencies such as France and Germany. There was little appreciation among British manufacturers for export of the direct effects of the rise of sterling in relation to the dollar upon export trade, and practically no attempt was made to measure this effect. The results of the policy being pursued to strengthen sterling were not viewed with alarm by British industry in general. The rise in sterling was viewed rather with satisfaction as an indication of returning economic power. Nevertheless, the pressure which the export industries began to feel in the latter part of 1924 was, in fact, a pressure due to the rising exchange, and not to a policy of credit restriction on the part of the City. While the rise of sterling was looked upon with surprising complacency upon the whole, there was a great deal of apprehension lest a policy of credit restriction should be inaugurated. There was a profound disinclination on the part of industry to undergo any further deflation to bring the pound back to parity. A deflationary monetary policy, it was felt, would discriminate against industrial in favour of City interests. But the feeling of divergence between the interests of industry and those of the City was not based upon an analysis of the real difference in the way the return to gold would affect industry and the City *in the short run*. It took the form of a rather vague feeling that the interests of the City, particularly the speculative part of the City community, were best served by a fluctuating exchange, while the best interests of industry were served by a stable exchange. The attitude of nervousness and apprehension on the part of industry over a possible hardening of money rates and credit contraction in connection with a return to gold was faithfully expressed by the public pronouncements of the Federation of British Industries. This is particularly well brought out in a communication addressed to the Government and to the Bank of England on 24 July, 1924, under the heading 'Industry and the Bank Rate'. This communication was drawn forth by fear of an increase in the bank rate to help bring the pound up to parity by a reduction of the British price level by about 10 per cent. To this the Federation, as 'the principal organization of British manufacturers', took strong exception and urged a waiting policy in the hope and belief that gold accumulation in America would inevitably force American prices up, and make British deflation unnecessary. The Federation sums up its plea against credit restriction as follows:

It appears to the Federation that any attempt to raise the real value of the pound sterling by 10 per cent by a process of arbitrary credit restriction would, in the present state of credit, and in view of the present trend of trade and prices in this country involve the most serious consequences to industry.

The immediate consequences of an increase in the value of a monetary unit, produced not by an increase in the efficiency of production, but by a manipulation of credit, are well known and generally admitted. They include, among others:

1. Serious temporary dislocation of trade and an increase in unemployment due to the effect upon producers, traders and buyers, of the *certainty* that the general level of prices will fall;
2. Severe industrial friction and dislocation, brought about by the fact that, in order that goods may be produced at the new lower level, all the items entering into the cost of production, including wages and salaries, must be adjusted to this level;
3. Severe loss to all holders of existing stocks of commodities, and to all who trade in borrowed money, i.e., virtually the whole trading and manufacturing community;
4. The strong probability of a severe check to export trade, since the improvement in the exchange value of sterling would be likely to precede and to move faster than the adjustment of internal prices.[1]

[1] This statement of the difficulties incident to a deflationary policy may be contrasted to the somewhat summary reference made to the same difficulties by the Committee on the Currency and Bank of England Note Issues, which says in Section 14 of its report:

We were satisfied that the mere announcement that the power to prohibit the export of gold would not be continued beyond 31 December, 1925, would automatically and rapidly bring about the credit conditions necessary to effect these adjustments (i.e. adjustment of internal purchasing power of the pound to its exchange value and restriction of foreign investments to export surplus) and that the effective gold standard could thus be restored *without further danger and inconvenience than that which is inevitable in any period of credit restriction and falling prices*. (Italics author's.)

The Committee, it will be recalled, was appointed in June, and the protest of the Federation of British Industries, which was not prepared to contemplate these 'dangers and inconveniences' in the same philosophic spirit was made at the end of July.

In stressing this last point in its indictment of a rapid return to parity, the Federation was in advance of the rank and file of industrial opinion. In view of this and similar pronouncements, it is not surprising that the subsequent course followed by the Bank of England in regard to money rates was felt by the Federation of British Industries to show a very considerable lack of appreciation of the difficulties faced by industry.

The special difficulties of the export trades during the rise of sterling gave rise to an unequal deflationary pressure, whose incidence was chiefly upon the exporters. This resulted in a general feeling of grievance on their part against the 'sheltered' industries, such for example, as municipal undertakings. These undertakings, it was felt, not being subject to foreign competition were able to keep up their prices. By doing so they increased the costs of the export industries in so far as these had to buy from sheltered industries. In addition they were able to maintain higher wage scales, thus causing inequalities and discontent among workers, and increasing the difficulties of exporters and manufacturers for export in paring down their costs.[1] The necessity for so doing may be illustrated by quoting from the speech of Lord Inchcape before the Annual Meeting of the shareholders of the P. & O. Steam Navigation Co. on 10 December, 1924. It is quite in line with what has been said above that Lord Inchcape did not once refer to the increased exchange value of the pound as a cause of the exporters' troubles, but laid them all at the door of labour. In fact, he passed over the whole exchange question with the simple statement that 'a resumption of a free market for gold would be good for trade and good for the City of London.' Whatever the defects of Lord Inchcape's speech from the point of view of the economist, it had the merit of reducing the exposition of the plight of the exporters to concrete figures, and it represented a large and important section of industrial opinion. As reported by *The Economist*, Lord Inchcape said, in part, that:

> Shipbuilding costs were still from 60 to 70 per cent above

[1] For a discussion of the relation between the 'sheltered' and 'unsheltered' industries in Great Britain, at this time, see 'Committee on Industry and Trade' – (the Balfour Committee), *Survey of Industrial Relations*, Introduction, esp. pp. 5–10, in which the relative position of the workers in the two types of industry is shown to have been much better in 1924 in the 'sheltered' than in the 'unsheltered' trades.

pre-war level, mainly through high wages and low output in the shipbuilding and contributory trades, while overhead charges in yards not fully employed were a serious cost factor. Continuing, he quoted figures taken from British and foreign tenders for railway material to illustrate the difficulty British manufacturers had as against Continental manufacturers in competing for orders for their factories and employment for their work-people. For wheels and axles, the highest British and Continental tenders were respectively: British, £1,350, Continental, £800; the lowest tenders: British, £920, Continental, £678. For steel tyres for locomotives, the highest tenders were: British, £1,988, Continental, £1,531. For steel springs the highest tenders were: British, £2,040, Continental, £1,706; the lowest: British, £1,463, Continental, £978. The lowest tenders for locomotive boilers were: British, £94,691, Continental, £54,695. These samples, he said, could be multiplied. The current f.o.b. quotations for English bar iron were £8. 2s. 6d. to £9. 16s. 6d. against for Continental bar iron £5. 10s. to £5. 12s. 6d. He believed, however, that prices were rising, as Continental firms found they were working at a serious loss.

In London and the outports used by the P. & O., the cost of loading and discharging showed a percentage increase of about 131 per cent over pre-war charges; in Antwerp it was a little over 49 per cent. Port dues in London had advanced 63 per cent, their coal now cost 80 per cent to 90 per cent more than in pre-war days. These increases had resulted from higher cost of labour. Production costs must be reduced in order that our export trade might revive.[1]

The examples cited by Lord Inchcape, as he said, could have been multiplied in the various export trades of England. The coal owners estimated that the return to parity meant for them a reduction of 1s. per ton approximately in the price they could get for exported coal.[2] Mr Keynes did not weary in pointing

[1] *The Economist*, 13 December, 1924, p. 972.

[2] This was one of the important factors in leading Sir Josiah Stamp to conclude that a large part of the depression in the coal industry was due to the policy of the return to gold. The view is expressed in his *Addendum to the Report of the Court of Inquiry Concerning the Coal Mining Dispute* appointed in 1925. Even the body of the report finds reduction in the price of exported coal a major factor in the troubles of the industry. Cmd. 2478.

out that the overvaluation of the pound meant directly reductions in prices realizable by exporters, and did not permit the part played by exchange fluctuations in the troubles of exporters to be overlooked or forgotten.[1] That such a situation called for an adjustment did not need to be debated. This adjustment could come either from the exchange side or from the side of prices. The rise of the Bank of England rate to 5 per cent on 5 March, 1925, in answer to the increase in the Federal Reserve Bank rate was clear notice that it was the policy of the Government and the Bank that it should come in prices. And on account of the different positions of the industries engaged in domestic business, in re-export business and in completely 'unsheltered' export business it was bound to be unequal in time and in its incidence.[2] It must increase unemployment during the period necessary to bring about a better equilibrium between the various parts of the British economy, including agriculture, in a new level of money incomes and prices. It was the anticipated increase in unemployment that was so greatly stressed by Mr Keynes in his criticisms of the prevailing policy. After the bank rate increase in March, this same anticipation brought Sir Alfred Mond into the field against the early return to gold. On 26 March, 1925, at the end of an earnest plea for a plan designed to reduce unemployment in the export industries with Government aid, he concluded as follows:

> Now, apparently, we are to be harnessed to the money rate in New York, our trade to be further depressed whenever there is a flurry on Wall Street, because some people seem to think that we must be hanged on a cross of gold. I hope that doctrine will be repudiated. I can imagine nothing more dangerous to the harassed and already depressed trade of this country than that we should hitch ourselves on to the American money market, and take it as the guide and goal and lodestar of British finance. We have deliberately adopted a policy which, undoubtedly, economically must produce a reduction of employment and a reduction of trade.[3]

[1] E.g., Articles in the *Evening Standard*, subsequently included in *The Economic Consequences of Mr Churchill*.

[2] J. M. Keynes, *The Economic Consequences of Mr Churchill*, (London, 1925) pp. 12–13 (See Essay 1).

[3] 182 *H.C. Deb. 5s.*, pp. 786–7.

Notwithstanding the undoubted difficulties of the export industries, however, no drastic action was taken to reduce costs till after the return to gold. The majority of manufacturers were not particularly interested in the question of gold and monetary policy. They did not very clearly relate it to their own practical problems. There was a natural desire on the part of the manufacturers that if there were to be changes in prices and exchange rates, these should be favourable to industry. There did exist in some cases a strong but not publicly expressed desire not merely for a stable but for a falling exchange rate. On the other hand, there was a strong and far more generally shared sentiment that it would be to the best interests of trade, and conformable to the national dignity to 'go back to the old standard, and stick to it through thick and thin'. Many important industrial leaders were thoroughly in accord with the policy of the Government and the Bank – taking the long view of the situation and falling in with the prevailing City opinion.

Agnostic as was the general attitude of industry towards monetary policy, and varied as were its views when these were actually expressed upon the problem, one common feeling began to pervade the whole of industry as 1924 drew to a close. Towards the end of the period of the rise of the pound, the prevailing industrial opinion was that the prime necessity was the removal of uncertainty from the situation. Business wanted to know where it stood. There began to be a fairly appreciable impression that perhaps, after all, the arguments advanced by Mr Keynes against the gold standard might have something in them. There was a growing insistence that these doubts as to the future be removed. On 18 March, 1925, the Federation of British Industries addressed an urgent appeal to the Chancellor of the Exchequer, a few words of which may be quoted:

It is . . . of such importance to all engaged in industry, both employers and employed, that the present uncertainty should be dispelled, and that industry should be able to make its plans for the immediate future with a definite knowledge of the general monetary conditions to be anticipated, that the advantages of an early declaration by His Majesty's Government would seem to outweigh the objections which might in more ordinary circumstances be urged against such a course.[1]

Similar views were expressed by other bodies. The Manchester Association of Importers and Exporters, for example, addressed a similar letter to the Chancellor on 21 April, 1925. Thus there was added to the pressure for an immediate decision brought to bear by the Dominions, a similar demand from large sections of the business community in England. There is no doubt that this domestic pressure for a decision was an important element in forcing the Government not to delay action.

When the return to gold actually became a fact the industrial world was given the certainty it desired. It began a more rigorous examination of costs of production, the results of which were soon apparent in the figures of unemployment. The table shows the course of unemployment by industries during 1925. The adjustments following the adoption of the gold standard are unmistakable. Although the total of unemployed at the end of the year was less than at the beginning there was a sharp increase in June and the peak of unemployment was reached in August. The changes in the employment of coal miners were by far the most important single item, and the effects of the decrease of export orders for coal are clearly reflected in the figures. The general tendency in unemployment in the so-called sheltered industries was downwards, but the unsheltered industries were obliged to make very radical adjustments after the return to gold, particularly the coal-mining and textile industries. The figures in the table tell a large part of the story of industrial and labour opposition to the time and manner of the return to gold.

Like the rank and file of business men, the rank and file of Labour, and of Labour leaders, were not very much interested in the problem of the return to gold. The Labour movement was, in general, opposed to deflationary policies of any kind, as tending to increase unemployment. But there was a section of labour and socialist opinion which felt that the power of credit control lodged in the banks, and in particular in the Bank of

[1] *The Times*, 19 March, 1925, p. 20.

GREAT BRITAIN AND NORTHERN IRELAND

PERCENTAGE UNEMPLOYED AMONG WORKPEOPLE INSURED AGAINST UNEMPLOYMENT UNDER THE UNEMPLOYMENT INSURANCE ACT

Trades	Jan. 26	Feb. 23	Mar. 23	Apr. 27	May. 25	June. 22	July. 27	Aug. 24	Sept. 26	Oct. 24	Nov. 28	Dec. 21
Unsheltered:												
Coal Mining	7·6	10·4	11·8	11·6	15·8	25·0	14·6	22·2	23·2	19·9	15·3	11·3
Iron and Steel Trades	27·3	22·8	23·9	26·7	23·6	24·7	25·0	25·9	25·7	24·3	23·6	24·4
Engineering	12·3	11·8	11·5	11·5	11·0	11·0	11·4	11·8	11·6	11·3	11·3	11·0
Shipbuilding	34·3	33·0	33·2	31·4	31·5	32·8	33·1	33·5	33·9	37·0	37·6	36·9
Woollen and Worsted Trade	12·0	13·5	14·0	16·6	17·8	19·7	21·3	18·1	13·0	10·8	9·6	8·8
Cotton Trade	6·2	6·8	7·2	7·1	7·6	8·7	11·6	13·6	10·2	7·0	6·7	6·7
Seamen	23·2	21·6	20·4	21·0	20·8	20·0	20·5	20·6	19·9	20·5	20·9	20·6
Dock Labourers	27·5	30·4	31·1	31·1	32·6	30·7	29·6	29·6	30·1	30·0	29·6	25·9
Sheltered:												
Boot and Shoe Industry	11·0	9·5	9·2	10·2	10·1	10·2	11·8	12·5	13·1	10·5	9·4	8·5
Printing and Bookbinding	5·9	6·0	6·1	5·4	5·1	4·9	4·6	4·5	4·3	4·2	4·1	3·8
Paper Manufacture	7·5	7·5	7·8	7·0	7·4	6·7	6·9	7·2	6·7	5·9	5·6	5·5
Building Trades	13·2	11·7	9·5	8·3	7·5	7·5	8·2	8·1	8·9	9·7	11·2	13·4
Railways	7·1	6·8	6·5	6·2	6·0	5·5	5·6	5·7	5·8	6·7	7·0	6·4
Gas, Water and Electric Supply Industries	6·9	6·6	6·5	6·4	6·1	5·9	5·7	5·8	6·1	5·9	5·8	5·7
Distributive Trades	7·5	7·7	7·5	7·2	6·7	6·3	6·2	6·4	6·6	6·2	6·3	5·6
Commercial, Banking, Insurance and Finance	6·3	6·2	6·0	5·9	5·4	4·9	4·8	4·6	4·9	3·2	3·2	3·1
Total Percentage of Unemployed	11·5	11·6	11·4	11·2	11·2	12·2	11·5	12·5	12·4	11·4	11·0	10·5

1925

Compiled from *Ministry of Labour Gazette*.

England, was not being used for the best interests of the nation, but to further the interests of financial groups. Of those who held this view Mr H. N. Brailsford was the most outspoken and active in his opposition to the policy by which the restoration of the gold standard was being prepared for in 1924 and 1925. At the Labour Party Conference, held at Queen's Hall, London, at the time of the Labour Government's defeat in Parliament, Mr Brailsford presented the following resolution in behalf of the Independent Labour Party:

> This Conference further records its opinion that, in view of the power of the Bank of England to lessen by a scientific regulation of credit the disastrous booms and slumps and the unemployment which they bring in their train, the Government should immediately give their attention to the influence of monetary policy on trade, industry and unemployment. It asks that steps should be taken, by nationalizing the Bank of England and otherwise to insure that the control of credit is exercised in the public interest and not in the interest of powerful financial groups.[1]

This resolution was adopted and became therefore part of the official programme of the Labour Party – but at that time it was not very much more than a form of words representing no great or responsible section of labour opinion.

Mr Brailsford was not entirely alone, however, in laying at the door of the City of London many of the existing industrial difficulties. Some months earlier Mr G. D. H. Cole had launched a more specific attack upon the policy of a return to gold parity. In frankly advocating bank inflation and thus expressing openly what many others either wished for secretly or hinted at in more guarded and diplomatic terms, Mr Cole expressed himself in language far more picturesque and imaginative than that in which currency controversy is usually couched. In the *Morning Post* of 13 June, 1924, Mr Cole wrote:

> Are we not artificially manufacturing a good half of our present unemployment? . . . There are people who think it more important to maintain British *Commercial Credit* represented by the worship of par than to make British industry

[1] *The Times*, 10 October, 1924, p. 7.

prosper. The Treasury and the Banks appear to take this view. I do not. I want moderate bank inflation because I believe it will reduce it (the unemployment problem) to manageable proportions.

Mr Cole then continues:

There is a Great God named Par who is worshipped daily at the Treasury and in the magnificent temples the big five are erecting on every street. Par likes unemployment; it is his form of human sacrifice. And on Par's altars the Treasury daily burns incense in the form of currency and credit. Par is a great God and the Treasury is his Prophet. But he worships him in secrecy and in silence and the world knoweth it not – except the few who know too much and like the Tar Baby, 'ain't sayin' nuffin'.

The ablest leader of the Minority movement in the British Labour Party, Mr John Wheatley, also identified himself with the opposition to the deflationary policy pursued in preparation for the return to gold.[1]

These expressions from the left did not, however, represent the attitude of the Labour movement which was much more moderate. When it came to the test of opposition to the Gold Standard Act in the House of Commons, the amendment proposed by the Labour Party merely stated that the time was not ripe for the action taken. It ran as follows:

This House cannot *at present* assent to the second reading of a bill which by providing for a return to the gold standard *with undue precipitancy*, may aggravate the existing grave condition of unemployment and trade depression.[2]

Mr Philip Snowden in moving and urging the amendment was at pains to make it clear that he was, as always, in favour of a gold standard. 'We do not,' he said, 'by this amendment, oppose a return to the gold standard ... we register our protest against haste.'[3] Even Mr Lees Smith, who anticipated a

---

[1] Cf. for example, his attack on the raising of the Bank rate in March to 5 per cent – 181 *H.C. Deb. 5s.*, p. 1376.

[2] 183 *H.C. Deb. 5s.*, p. 625 – italics author's.

[3] Ibid., p. 626.

reduction of 5 per cent in British prices and feared that the price of a stable exchange would be that Englishmen would lose control of their own internal prices and become 'satellites of the American price level,'[1] merely advocated allowing the return to gold to come about automatically eight months later by letting the Gold and Silver (Export Control) Act expire at the end of the year.

The City of London was in favour of the return to the gold standard. It regarded its final restoration as a landmark in British history, a vindication of British financial integrity, and an assurance that British financial prestige and power would regain much that it had lost. It was on the basis of the last of these considerations that Mr Walter Leaf, Chairman of the Westminster Bank Ltd., had brought the question of an early return to gold into the foreground of discussion as early as August, 1924, just after the ratification of the Dawes plan. Under the terms of the Dawes report, the option was given to Germany to go on a gold or on a sterling exchange basis. The Federal Advisory Council in the United States issued a statement strongly urging the adoption by Germany of the gold exchange standard, on the ground that the adoption of a sterling-exchange standard would lead to instability of exchange.[2] Mr Leaf regarded this pronouncement as a serious challenge to the supremacy of the pound sterling. He took the position that a combination of the credit resources of the United States with the enterprise and world commerce of Germany, while the pound sterling remained depreciated in the markets of the world, might force England back to a gold standard whether she wished it or not.[3] He therefore boldly proposed that the Bank rate be increased to 5 per cent with a $3\frac{1}{2}$ per cent rate of interest on foreign balances if necessary, accompanied by a definite announcement of intention to return to gold on the part of the Government.

This proposal met with a very mixed reception in the City,[4] for though the opinion of the City was almost unanimously in favour of a return to gold there was still present a strong hope

[1] Ibid., p. 644.

[2] *Federal Reserve Bulletin*, (June 1924) p. 460.

[3] *Monthly Review* of the Westminster Bank, quoted in the *Bankers' Magazine*, (London, August 1924) p. 147.

[4] *The Economist*, (28 June, 1924) p. 1289.

that it could be brought about by inflation in America. There was also apprehension, lest, if achieved without a proper adjustment of price levels, it could not be maintained. In his speech to the shareholders of the Midland Bank in January, 1923, Mr McKenna had pointed out that when in April, 1920, England raised the Bank rate to 7 per cent, the pound was 3·88 and that after eighteen months deflation in concert with America the pound was about the same level, while beginning with the late summer of 1921 when America abandoned deflation and England continued it, it rose close to parity. Mr McKenna, at that time, felt that further deflation in England was unnecessary and hoped that the return to parity might be painlessly accomplished by American inflation alone if only England adopted a waiting policy. This optimistic view was still held in high quarters in the City a year later. Even when the 'flight from the pound' was in progress, Mr Goodenough, Chairman of Barclays Bank, said with reference to the gold standard:

> Before it can be achieved, there must be a further fall in prices in this country or an advance of prices in America. The latter of these alternatives is so evidently a possibility that from this point of view alone we should be justified in avoiding action designed to force down prices in this country . . . till the tendency in America is more clearly defined.[1]

The waiting attitude long adopted by some of the leaders of British banking and reflected in these speeches was not entirely discarded at the time of Mr Leaf's call for drastic action. Even in January, 1925, just before the actual return, the City did not speak with unanimity and decision in favour of immediate action at whatever cost. For example, in his speech to the shareholders of the District Bank Ltd., on 23 January, 1925, Sir Christopher Needham said:

> It is earnestly to be hoped that the decision (to return to the gold standard) will not come till it is clear that the approximation of the pound to parity arises from the establishing of satisfactory trade balances. It would be little short of disaster if, after the return to the gold standard, it became necessary,

[1] Address to Shareholders of Barclays Bank, January, 1924. *The Economist* (26 January, 1924) p. 153.

in order to protect our gold supply, to raise rates to an extent which might press unduly upon commerce.

When it became apparent that the hope of price inflation in America was, in fact, illusory, and that the price of further deflation in England would have to be paid for a return to the gold standard, the City was prepared to have England pay that price. If there were a definitive choice to be made between stable exchange and stable prices, the City was on the whole prepared to choose stable exchange. 'Stabilization,' said Sir Charles Addis, Director of the Bank of England and Chairman of the Hongkong and Shanghai Banking Corporation, 'is not a function of the gold standard. What the gold standard does is to link our prices to world prices,'[1] and Sir Charles Addis was one of the most uncompromising supporters of the gold standard. The governing consideration in the minds of those urging an early return was that, in their view, the re-establishment of a free market for gold in London was essential for the maintenance of British credit throughout the world. The restoration of confidence in the pound sterling and in the willingness and ability of London to pay its obligations in gold on demand were felt to be imperative if London was to hold and increase the volume of financial business that had in the past made it the greatest of all financial centres. Upon this confidence depended therefore, in large measure, the preservation intact of a large part of the invisible exports of England. There had been during the post-war years after the deflation a very marked reduction in the volume of bills in the London money market, and this deficiency, even after allowing for the rise in prices, was still a fact of importance at the time of resumption. Lack of bills was to the London money market analogous to lack of orders to the export trade. The return to the gold standard was also felt to be essential in order that London might maintain its importance as a grantor of foreign loans, for upon these in the future as in the past, the continued growth of English trade would largely depend. This meant taking the long run view of the national advantage, a view characteristic of English financial leaders, and well expressed by Mr F. C. Goodenough in the following words:

[1] *Bankers' Magazine*, (January, 1924) p. 22.

We have to pay our debts abroad, and we have to purchase raw material from abroad, and if we are to provide markets for our manufacturers and promote the production of raw materials for them to deal with, we have also to invest capital abroad. The uncertainty involved in dealing with these matters will be less if our currency is at parity than if it is at a fluctuating discount in foreign markets, and these considerations outweigh any temporary advantages which might accrue to us through a depreciated currency.[1]

Even Mr McKenna, whose criticisms of the lack of elasticity in the British banking system and of Bank of England policy were often severe, marshalled the arguments in favour of a gold standard. It possesses, in his view, three cardinal advantages: first, it establishes an international standard of value acceptable by the whole world; second, it is automatic and relieves the Central Bank of responsibilities which might not be wisely used, but still leaves some scope for management; and third, and greatest of all, is its moral effect. So long as nine people out of ten think it is the best, it is the best.

These and other[2] considerations were advanced by spokesmen for the gold standard, and they represented the predominating, the orthodox, and in the end the prevailing view. It was a characteristic of this view that it looked past the temporary adjustments involved in the return to gold to the lasting benefits beyond. It was not only in keeping with the financial tradition of London to do so, but it was also relatively easier for the City to take a philosophic view of the necessary adjustments

[1] Speech to the shareholders of Barclay's Bank, London, *The Economist*, (24 January, 1925) p. 151.

[2] Mr. A. W. Kiddy, editor of the London *Bankers' Magazine*, in the course of a missionary speaking trip to the industrial provincial cities in behalf of the gold standard, emphasized in particular:
1. That other nations were expecting England to return to gold, and failure to do so would be a blow to English credit;
2. A return to gold would reveal the real balance of payments and would force public attention on the failure of British exports to compete;
3. It would facilitate foreign loans;
4. It would prevent future 'unsound' experiments by Socialist Governments which might divert the English people from the only real solution of their problems – economy and hard work.

Bankers' Magazine, (London, April, 1925) pp. 594–8.

involved. For considerations of the national welfare in the more distant future did not come into the same direct conflict with the immediate self-interest of many of the component parts of the London money market, as they did with that of large sections of industry and labour. In the case of acceptors and dealers and investors in bills, indeed, the restoration of the gold standard offered prospects of an early increase in the volume of their business.

Enough has been said to indicate that the opinions thus expressed did in fact represent a real conflict of economic interest. The policy of the Bank of England *did* involve a balancing of loss and gain between the entrepôt business and the export business of England, and between the effects of loss of confidence in British finance, and of restoration of that confidence. The immediate need of the export industries was a rate of exchange that would accurately reflect the parity between the purchasing power of the pound abroad and its purchasing power over material and labour at home. The immediate need of the London money market and the entrepôt trade was a rate of exchange restricted in its fluctuations by gold points so as to provide a stable medium for the transaction of its business as financier and middleman for the trade of the world. The ultimate need of the nation was an adjustment and reconciliation between these two. Since considerations of confidence, of sentiment and of prestige were sufficient to compel the decision that these gold points should be the old gold points and the new par should be the old par, this reconciliation had to come about through price deflation.

The return to a gold standard was accomplished in England at a great cost and by an effort which embraced not only a policy of heavy taxation and resistance to price inflation at home, but also difficult and long sustained financial diplomacy in the Empire and on the Continent. If the return to gold meant no more than stable exchanges at the sacrifice of stable internal prices in England, the advantages would not have been commensurate with the cost. To make them so, the second great element in British financial policy, the stabilization of the value of gold had to be realized.[1] This meant that the burden of

[1] The perfunctory debate on the Gold Standard Act, 1925, in the House of Commons contained only one speech emphasizing this point. This was a very

administration and responsibility placed upon the central banking authority was not, as Mr McKenna suggested, greatly diminished by the return to gold. It meant that in certain eventualities movements of gold would give the signal for action to the central banking authorities, confirming or correcting their own unsupported judgement. It meant also that certain very powerful financial tools were placed in their hands in the administration of a policy directed towards stability of prices. It meant that popular confidence was restored and that their work would not be disturbed by sudden panics and unreasoned fears. It did not mean that the steps taken by the leading financial countries in the world in learning to control their money and credit were to be retraced and the welfare of millions abandoned to the vagaries of nature in yielding abundance or scarcity of gold. The choice between stabilization of prices and stabilization of exchange was met by Mr Keynes by choosing stabilization of prices. This was in a sense a defeatist choice. For it abandoned one half of the objective. A policy of maintaining a gold standard plus stabilization of the value of gold aims to achieve the whole. Stabilization of the value of gold means continual reference to some outside criterion. That criterion can only be the general level of prices in the great trading countries.

---

able statement by Mr Boothby who pointed out that 'as a result of the step the Government have taken we are now in a position to put into effect the Genoa resolutions on currency.' The conclusion of Mr Boothby's speech is very pertinent to the discussion in the text and runs as follows:

It depends on what the Chancellor of the Exchequer's motive is in having taken this step whether the fear that some of us have entertained about this return to the gold standard will be realized or not. Is his motive to return automatically to the pre-war gold standard and that our credit policy should be influenced entirely in relation to the reserve of gold in the Bank of England? If this is the case then I think we run a real danger, and I think he has taken a direct step back. But if, as I am perfectly certain is really the case after listening to his speech, he has taken this step in order to provide a basis for a new currency system, then I think we may say that he has laid the foundation stone for that new international economic structure which we must build up in the next fifteen or twenty years.

183 *H.C. Deb.* 5*s.*, pp. 695–7.

3 The Origins of Cheap Money, 1931-1932[1]

EDWARD NEVIN

[This article was first published in *Economica*, (February 1953).]

I

Any study of the British cheap money policy must obviously begin with a definition of the term 'cheap money'. This is impossible in any absolute sense, since the term is essentially and necessarily comparative. It can refer only to a structure of interest rates possessing a basis lower than either what is considered 'natural' or 'right' – standards which are in themselves not easily defined – or, more commonly, lower than that which has existed over a fairly substantial period in the recent past. The phrase is used in its second sense in what follows referring to the means adopted by the monetary authorities in 1932 to achieve and maintain a level of interest rates lower than that which had been usual in the years prior to 1932. For practical purposes, this means the attainment of a gilt-edged rate of $3\frac{1}{2}$ per cent or below; but this absolute measure cannot be applied in any rigid way. In the conditions of 1932, a gilt-edged rate of $3\frac{1}{2}$ per cent was regarded as low primarily because the average rate during the preceding decade had been close to 5 per cent. After a period of many years during which the gilt-edged rate had remained around $2\frac{1}{2}$ per cent, a rate of $3\frac{1}{2}$ per cent would obviously not be regarded as low; what is 'cheap' money is conditional upon the prevailing attitudes of the public, and these in turn are governed by what has come to be regarded as usual, and possibly by what is regarded as appropriate for the particular circumstances of the time. Views as to the cheapness or otherwise of money, as with other things, depend upon

[1] This article is a by-product of research carried out with the aid of a Houblon-Norman Fellowship; my thanks are therefore due to the Trustees of the Houblon-Norman Fund. It owes much to my teachers, Professors Sir Dennis Robertson and R. F. Kahn, and also to the expert and generous criticism of Mr H. G. Johnson of King's College, Cambridge.

the relationship of its price to current demand as well as to previous prices.

A *policy* of cheap money implies conscious operation on the part of the monetary authorities aimed at the achievement of low interest rates, as opposed to the case where interest rates are low as a result of changes which are attributable only incidentally and partially to government action. Interest rates may fall as a result of a lowered desire on the part of the public to hold wealth in the form of cash, possibly but not necessarily caused by a smaller requirement of cash as a result of falling output and prices. Government policies, or the lack of them, may well be responsible for this, and therefore for the low interest rates which follow. But the cheap money would be a by-product, whether desired or not, of a wider process and would not in itself be the aim of policy. And, of course, such changes may occur quite independently of government action. Similarly, a country on the gold standard would normally experience a fall in interest rates when an influx of gold occurred, for whatever reason; such a fall could hardly be described as a cheap money policy. The latter term connotes measures taken by the authorities with the aim of low interest rates specifically in view, as part, doubtless, of a general economic or budgetary plan, but an aim of policy in its own right, nevertheless.

That such a conscious and deliberate policy was pursued in Britain during the 1930s does not necessarily mean, however, that the emergence of low interest rates in 1932 was solely and entirely due to action on the part of the authorities with the establishment of cheap money in view. Many characteristics of the British monetary system have been essentially empirical or even accidental in their origin; a subsidiary feature of a measure adopted to meet a certain requirement has been retained and has acquired a vital role in the monetary scheme long after the original requirement has been met and the corrective measure become unnecessary. It is argued below that the cheap money policy of the 1930s was of this kind; originally an off-shoot of foreign exchange policy, it survived the exchange problems of 1932 and flourished in its own right. But before developing this view, it is necessary to discuss how far cheap money was the result simply of the economic depression of the time.

II

In Table I are shown the movements in the price of various types of securities between August 1931 and July 1932. The remarkable rise in bond prices in the first half of 1932 is evident; it was this rise which made possible the great War Loan conversion announced at the end of June 1932, the landmark of the cheap money policy which continued until 1951. What are the factors which caused this recovery of the gilt-edged and bond markets from the low levels reached in September 1931?

TABLE I: SECURITY PRICE INDICES*

		Gilt-edged	Industrial Fixed-interest	Ordinary (general)
1931	August	97.2	92·5	73·0
	September	86·9	86·7	78·3
	October	94·3	92·6	87·4
	November	92·8	89·8	79·6
	December	91·3	86·3	73·7
1932	January	94·8	86·8	75·8
	February	97·5	88·1	76·1
	March	101·9	93·9	80·0
	April	101·4	93·0	70·4
	May	105·8	95·6	65·1
	June	107·3	93·4	67·1
	July	116·7	105·0	76·4

* *Source:* Bank of England *Statistical Summary.*

Three possible factors may underly such a sudden and sustained movement in security prices:

1. a fall in the public demand (including the demand of foreigners) for cash and a rise in their demand for less liquid assets;
2. an increase in the quantity of money, all other things remaining equal;
3. a switch of invested funds out of equity securities and into fixed-interest securities.

The third factor can be dismissed fairly briefly. It is often said that in times of depression, when profit expectations are low, investors will tend to transfer their wealth from unremunerative equities and purchase gilt-edged bonds carrying a guaranteed return.[1] While this may be generally true, it is certainly not the explanation of the beginning of cheap money in 1931–2; in September, 1931, indeed, the reverse occurred. The collapse of the pound gave rise to some expectation of inflation in Britain, and the equity market benefited in its role as an inflation hedge.[2] Between December 1931 and March 1932, when the great transformation in the gilt-edged market occurred,[3] ordinary shares actually rose, so that the rise in the one market is hardly attributable to widespread switching from the other. Some recession occurred in equities in the second quarter of 1932, but this was little more than a return to the pre-crisis level. By July, indeed, the ordinary share market had recovered all the ground lost since 1931.

Examination of the second factor is equally unconvincing. The recovery of December 1931 – March 1932 occurred at a time when bank deposits were actually *falling;* the average (weekly) deposits of the London Clearing Banks fell from £1,724 million in October 1931 to £1,676 million in March 1932. Thereafter, a substantial credit expansion occurred, as is easily seen from the bank statistics, and this undoubtedly assisted in the further advance of the gilt-edged market. The initial rise in gilt-edged, however, in the early part of 1932, was clearly not the result of an expansion in the volume of money. To find the explanation of the original upward trend in gilt-edged at the end of 1931 and early in 1932, therefore, recourse must be had to the first factor; expressed briefly, a change in the public's liquidity-preference.

III

This factor may be considered under the two separate headings corresponding to the Keynesian terminology: (*a*) the public's transactions (and precautionary) demand; (*b*) the speculative demand. The latter may, again for convenience, be sub-divided into the speculative attitude of British residents on the one hand

---

[1] See, e.g., Hawtrey: *A Century of Bank Rate*, V, pp. 149–50; Grant: *The Post-War Capital Market*, III, p. 51, and XVI, p. 298; Kock: *A Study of Interest Rates*, VII, p. 124; Crowther: *An Outline of Money* (1940), VI, p. 212.

[2] See W. A. Brown: *The International Gold Standard Reinterpreted*, Vol. II, ch. 31, pp. 1094–5.

[3] The continuous recovery in gilt-edged began in the second week of December 1931.

and foreigners (using the word in its widest sense) on the other.

Whatever the terminology employed, there can be found in many authorities the view that the low levels of prices and output characteristic of a depression will of themselves, and quite apart from action by the monetary authorities, cause interest rates to fall and an era of cheap money to begin. Marshall attributes this primarily to the low prices themselves:

> I myself go with those who hold that the statistics bear out the *a priori* probability that, first, the rates of discount would generally be higher when prices are rising than when they are falling, because the borrowers would be eager for loans; and, secondly, that they would generally be higher during periods of high prices than in periods of low prices.[1]

Hawtrey stresses also the effect of low prices upon the demand for credit:

> It should be observed that, quite apart from any deliberate action by bankers, there is in any case an important influence at work to lower the rate of interest. ... Falling prices of themselves make borrowing less attractive and reduce the rate of interest which borrowers are willing to pay.[2]

The same writer, in another place, uses a much wider phrase: 'When, as is usual, cheap money and depression go together. ...'[3] Pigou associates low interest rates during a depression with the low level of entrepreneurs' expectations;[4] Haberler, in more modern terminology, ascribes the fall in interest rates to a superfluity of credit over the public's demand for cash balances.[5]

There is, therefore, a considerable body of authority to support the view that cheap money follows inevitably from depression conditions. It is difficult, however, to ascribe the fall in interest rates during the first half of 1932 wholly to a fall in

[1] Evidence before the Committee on Indian Currency, Q. 11679, *Official Papers*, p. 274. See also *Money, Credit and Prices*, II, i, 4, p. 74 and IV, iv, p. 257.
[2] *Currency and Credit*, I, p. 12; and also IV, p. 57.
[3] *A Century of Bank Rate*, VI, p. 168.
[4] *Industrial Fluctuations*, III, p. 33.
[5] *Prosperity and Depression* (1937 ed.) ch. 10, p. 286; see also Kock: op. cit., VII, p. 124; Grant, op. cit., III, p. 48; Hallowell: *A Study of British Interest Rates*. I, p. 8.

prices and output. In Table II below the price and output movements are shown for the six months preceding the crucial
period (early December 1931 – March 1932) when gilt-edged
began their recovery, and for the months immediately following.

TABLE II. THE VALUE OF OUTPUT, JULY 1931–JUNE 1932

| | Board of Trade Indices[1] | | |
	Industrial Production (1)	Wholesale Prices (2)	Index of value of output (1 × 2) (3)
July–September 1931	89·3	100·3	89·6
October–December 1931	97·1	105·5	102·4
January–March 1932	95·1	105·2	100·0
April–June 1932	94·3	100·4	94·7

The calculation of the value of output can obviously be only
a rough guide to movements in the transactions demand for
cash, but it affords some indication. The notable fact brought
out by the table is that during the last quarter of 1931 the value
of output (and, by implication, the transactions demand for
cash) had risen quite substantially. A relatively small decrease
occurred in the first half of 1932, and this no doubt offset to
some degree the fall in bank deposits previously mentioned.
But in the months in which the initial recovery occurred in the
gilt-edged market the data lend little support to the view that
the fall in interest rates resulted from a lower transactions
demand for cash. What other evidence is available tends to
reinforce the implications of Table II. In Table III indices are
shown of the note circulation and of the level of bank clearings
which show the same pattern.

TABLE III. NOTE CIRCULATION AND BANK CLEARINGS[2]

		Index of Note Circulation	Index of Bank Clearings
1931	July–September	93·1	83·3
	October–December	95·5	88·3
1932	January–March	93·9	90·7
	April–June	92·8	85·2

[1] Source: Bank of England *Statistical Summary*.
[2] Source: Bank of England *Statistical Summary*. Both series seasonally corrected.
The bank clearings shown are the total Metropolitan, Country and Provincial
clearings.

Even after eliminating the seasonal rise which normally occurs in these months, both series had risen rather than fallen in the last quarter of 1931, which does not suggest that the transactions demand for cash had fallen.

IV

The search for the cause of the initial fall in the gilt-edged rate in 1931–2 is therefore narrowed down to the second component in the public's demand for cash – the speculative demand. Here, in the nature of the case, evidence can only be suggestive rather than conclusive. But there are many indications that the state of public confidence had improved substantially during the weeks in which the gilt-edged recovery began, so that it is difficult to resist the conclusion that the one was the cause of the other. It is convenient to consider firstly the state of confidence of the British public itself.

To every action there is an equal and opposite reaction. After the disastrous collapse of sterling in September 1931 the mere passage of time, and the fact that the worst had happened, were bound to mean some degree of recovery in the security markets. The bears cover their positions and strengthen prices somewhat;[1] panic hoards of cash begin to trickle back into the market. A technical recovery of this kind, without support from exogenous factors, will invariably follow a crisis, although it may not lift prices very far.

This natural process received assistance, however, from the far-reaching political consequences of the September crisis. It had been a widespread belief in the financial world that the Labour Government had been at least partly responsible for the collapse.[2] It was replaced by a government of a political hue more acceptable in the City,[3] and one which, furthermore, was widely believed to be committed to severe conditions attached

[1] See, for example, Brown, op. cit., p. 1101: 'The export of British capital from August to 21 September had been considerable, but in less than two weeks after the suspension (of convertibility) this movement was reversed. ... The main influence, however, in strengthening the pound was the covering of the bear positions built up before 21 September, which amounted to between £40 million and £60 million'. This, of course, refers to the foreign exchange market, but it illustrates the forces at work.

[2] See, for example, *The Economist*, (22 August, 1931) p. 339.

[3] See Hallowell, op. cit., I, p. 8.

to the American and French loans,[1] and to a modified form of the recommendations of the May Committee, all of which were regarded as essential to financial orthodoxy and the solvency of the economy.[2]

There is abundant evidence of the part played in the restoration of confidence by the accession to power of the National Government:

> But more important than anything else was the very existence of the National Government ... British business and financial interests felt more happy and optimistic to see people in whom they had confidence holding the reins of government.[3]

In a leading article, *The Times* declared,

> The strongest and simplest tribute to the quality of the electorate and to the policy of its National Government is that between them they have made conversion not only possible but inevitable.[4]

But the policy which had worked such wonders was, by almost any standards, a severely deflationary policy. It was the Spartan austerity of the Chancellor which had heartened the City.[5] This poses something of a dilemma. On the one hand,

---

[1] The 'bankers' ramp' controversy is admirably surveyed by Morton: *British Finance, 1930–40*, V, pp. 62–71.

[2] 'In view of the prevailing conception of 'sound' public finance among British public opinion, and the business world in particular, the determined stand of the National Government by the principles of financial orthodoxy had a favourable psychological influence' (Arndt: *Lessons of the 1930s*, IV, pp. 129–30). A further significant point was that the policy of the National Government seemed to be following the lines suggested in Addendum I of the Macmillan Report, which advocated an all-round reduction in money incomes (Cmd. 3897, especially pp. 198–200). The unduly high level of rentier incomes had been deplored (para. 28), and the need for lower interest rates stressed. Conversion of War Loan therefore became a possibility for what were partly political reasons. (I am indebted to Prof. R. S. Sayers for drawing my attention to this important point.)

[3] Morton, op. cit., XIV, pp. 247–8. The *Bankers' Magazine* went further: 'It cannot be too clearly recognized that but for the substitution of the National for the Socialist government ... it would have been quite impossible for the conversion operation to have been carried through successfully' (August 1932, p. 179).

[4] *The Times*, (1 July, 1932).

[5] The *Investors' Chronicle* of 14 May, 1932 for example, remarked (p. 964) that 'Mr Neville Chamberlain's speech at the annual dinner of the British Bankers'

the circumstances of 1932 indicated the necessity of a policy of cheap money; on the other hand, the psychological state of the investing public was clearly such that a deflationary purgation was essential before cheap money became at all a practical proposition. As Pigou remarks:

> If business men at home believe that a country is going to the dogs on account of extravagant consumption, an economy campaign may restore their confidence and so cause the demand schedule to rise. . . . Thus it is not certain that in the first stages of the 1930 panic the Government's economy campaign was a mistake.[1]

The effect of the policy of the National Government, therefore, however deficient in some directions by modern standards, must not be overlooked in this matter of the recovery of business confidence and the first stirrings of cheap money. There can be little doubt that the personalities and policy of the Government helped to restore confidence in the minds of both domestic and foreign investors.[2] The results of the recovery of international confidence in sterling are discussed below, but it is important to note that they were ante-dated by the results at home, which formed the necessary basis upon which the cheap money policy was built.

Association made a good impression. *His forecast of further drastic economies was particularly welcomed*, and has contributed to the strength of British Government stocks . . .' Of Mr Chamberlain's budget in 1932 the National City Bank of New York had observed in its circular for April that 'it must be regarded as heroic devotion to a sound principle that any provision for the sinking fund should be made in a year of such stress.' The sum of £32·5 million was set aside for this purpose.

[1] *Keynes's 'General Theory'*, XI, p. 41.

[2] A further factor, in the case of foreigners, was undoubtedly the announcement at the end of October 1931 that the Bank of England had arranged to repay £20 million of its international credits before the due date. See Brown, op. cit., p. 1102, and *The Economist*, (5 March, 1932) p. 507. The height of bank rate – maintained at 6 per cent from September 1931 to February 1932 – was also a reviver apparently for both domestic and foreign confidence. It had the effect of quelling the misgivings of those who feared that the departure from gold 'might lead the pound along the path of the post-war mark and rouble' (Morton, op. cit., IX, p. 123). The *Bankers' Magazine* regarded a high bank rate as 'the only possible policy' for 'the maintenance of public confidence' (January 1932) p. 13.

V

A similar story can be told of the recovery of confidence in the pound on the part of foreigners. By the beginning of 1932 the wild retreat from sterling had been replaced by a movement into it. This may have been due to the belief that sterling had endured its ordeal, and would now remain unscathed while other currencies were put to the test. It was no doubt partly due to the fact that London was still a leading financial centre in the world, and that for many purposes sterling balances were still a great convenience. Whatever the reason, an observer was able to remark early in 1932 that '(the world's) confidence in the solidity of England's position has shown a remarkable revival.'[1] And another: 'Early in the New Year, however, the tide turned, and foreign short money began to return to London. This brought the British authorities face to face with another problem, namely, that of preventing an over-rapid and disruptive appreciation of the pound.'[2]

The important fact as regards the cheap money policy is not so much this commencement of an inflow of foreign funds as its effect upon official credit policy. Had Britain been on the gold standard, the inflow of capital would in itself have reduced interest rates. In the absence of special action on the part of the Bank, the sellers of gold would have acquired from the Bank sterling resources with which to buy Treasury Bills or other gilt-edged securities. In order to induce existing holders to part with their securities, the rate of interest would have needed to fall sufficiently to induce them to move out of securities and into cash. The gold itself would have formed the basis for the expansion in the volume of credit.

With a non-convertible currency, however, this reasoning can no longer be applied. The sellers of gold can no longer legally demand sterling from the Bank of England in exchange for it – except, in 1932, at a rate far below the market price – and in order to obtain sterling the sellers would have to cause the sterling exchange rate to rise sufficiently to induce domestic holders of sterling to hold gold or foreign exchange instead.

---

[1] J. Henry Schroder & Co., *Quarterly Review*, (May, 1932) p. 171. See also Waight: *The Exchange Equalisation Account*, II, p. 8.

[2] *The Economist Banking Supplement*, 14 May, 1932) p. 6.

The foreigner's purchase of securities would, therefore, be offset by a corresponding sale by the erstwhile holders of sterling, the rate of interest remaining unaffected. The important difference between the two cases is that under the gold standard the inflow of capital provides the basis for extra credit, while under an inconvertible currency the foreigner can only obtain sterling which someone else has given up. In the former case, therefore, the impact is felt on the interest rate level, while in the latter case it is the exchange rate which moves to achieve equilibrium. Interest rates would be affected in this latter case only with the special assumption of sterling being transferred from a domestic idle deposit to an active deposit held by the foreigner, or *vice versa*, while adjustments between various types of market will occur if the transfer is effected from one type of security to another. There is no particular reason for supposing that these special considerations materially affected the situation in early 1932.

All this presupposes, however, that the monetary authorities play a purely neutral role. This was certainly not true in Britain at this time. Having experienced the sudden devaluation of 1931, the authorities appear to have been most anxious to prevent sterling appreciation, signs of which appeared early in 1932. This seems to have been due partly to a belief that devaluation had turned out to be a blessing in disguise to British exports, but mainly to the fear – which proved to be well-founded – that the appreciation would be essentially transitory, and would lead before long to another depreciation of sterling with potentialities of another September crisis. Hence, one writer remarked that 'the problem is how to keep the pound from rising at too rapid a rate to be healthy'.[1] There were two ways in which this appreciation of sterling was opposed, and it was as a by-product of these steps that the beginnings of the official cheap money policy emerge. One was to offset the pressure on sterling by official purchases of foreign currencies, and the other was to attempt to check the inflow at its source by reducing the interest-rate gap which was at least partly the

---

[1] S. Montagu & Co., *Weekly Review*, (31 March, 1932); quoted by Brown, op. cit., p. 1106. Hall also suggests that the absence of forward buying indicates the highly speculative nature of much of the inflow – *The Exchange Equalisation Account*, IV, pp. 37–8. See also Morton, op. cit., IX, p. 125.

explanation of sterling's attractiveness to some foreign investors.

The activities of the Bank of England under the first heading may be seen from Chart I. Foreign currencies seem to have

——————— Banking Dept's Security Holdings (left-hand scale)

— — — — — Issue Dept's 'other securities' Holdings (right-hand scale)

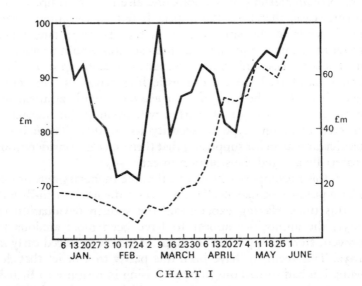

CHART I

been held under the heading 'other securities' in the Issue Department, since operations on the foreign exchanges were said to be suitable only for official account, and unsuitable for the Banking Department.[1] It will be seen that the main accumu-

[1] Many leading authorities suggest this. It is clearly implied by Hall, op. cit., IV, pp. 34, 44–5; Truptil (*British Banks*, I, p. 45) states that 'The foreign currencies and foreign securities acquired by the Bank in 1932 materially assisted in swelling this figure' (i.e. 'other securities'); Brown, op. cit., ch. 31, p. 1109, states that 'This foreign exchange was included in the item 'other securities' in the Issue Department'. The same writer quotes the weekly reviews of S. Montagu & Co.: 'The heavy increase of £12,035,388 in Other Securities . . . is attributable to foreign exchange transactions . . .' (12 May, 1932); 'Other Securities have risen £8,896,857 presumably owing to foreign exchange transactions' (2 June, 1932). The Banking Department seems to have indulged, perhaps temporarily, in the purchase of foreign exchange despite its alleged unsuitability – see the same company's review of 21 April, 1932, Brown, Ibid., p. 1110.

lation occurred in March and May,[1] during which period 'other securities' rose some £53 million; in June, the main support seems to have been given *via* the gold market, while after June, of course, these functions were performed by the Exchange Equalization Account.[2]

The second course to be followed in order to check the inflow of funds was obviously the lowering of domestic interest rates. Provided that forward currency can be obtained, holders of short-term capital need not concern themselves with the possibility of exchange depreciation, since they can cover themselves against it. The cost of this cover, however, has to be deducted from interest rates obtainable in various centres, so that forward exchange rates can be said to be at their 'interest parities' when international short-term rates are brought to equality by the deduction of the cost of forward exchange cover expressed as a rate of interest.[3] There will, of course, be limits within which such rates may move because of the cost of transfer and administration, and the general inconvenience of having capital invested abroad rather than domestically.

Now the position in late 1931 and early 1932 was that a very wide gap existed between the yields obtainable from short-term funds in London and those in other financial centres, after allowance had been made for exchange cover. Table IV shows the position in detail for London as compared with New York and Paris. It will be seen that a wide gap persisted during the first quarter of 1932 in the case of London–Paris rates, and for

[1] This does not mean that no official purchases occurred before March. On the contrary, the activities of the 'special buyer' were noted in the foreign exchange market throughout February – see *The Economist*, 13 February, 1932, p. 380, 20 February, 1932, p. 437, 27 February, 1932, p. 490. The repayments of the foreign credits in early March 1932 also indicate foreign exchange operations in January and February. This is not discernible in the bank returns, presumably because the foreign exchange was being held on behalf of the Treasury by departmental funds.

[2] *The Economist* commented: 'In view of the trend of funds towards England it is not surprising that early this week the Bank announced that it had purchased £2,012,655 of bar gold and a further £967,899 on Thursday. It is not unlikely that these purchases represent transfers to the Bank from the Treasury, who may have previously purchased it in the guise of the 'unknown buyer' in the London market.' It criticized the Bank for buying devisen while the Treasury bought gold, and expressed satisfaction that the roles had apparently been reversed (21 May, 1932) p. 1129.

[3] Einzig: *Theory and Practice of Forward Exchange*, XVIII.

the first two quarters in the case of London–New York rates. By mid-1932 both gaps had disappeared.

TABLE IV. RETURN ON SHORT-TERM FUNDS IN LONDON VIS-À-VIS NEW YORK AND PARIS, 1931–2

Year	Qtr.	Average spot rate	3 months' forward covering		London Discount Rate[2]	Net Rate (4–3)	Foreign Discount Rate[2]	Gap (5–6)
			Av. cost[1]	As rate % p.a.				
		(1)	(2)	(3)	(4)	(5)	(6)	(7)
		London–New York						
		$	$	%	%	%	%	%
1931	1	4·857	0·0043	0·36	2·44	2·08	1·16	0·92
	2	4·863	0·0063	0·49	2·33	1·84	1·11	0·73
	3	4·466	0·0348	3·12	3·58	0·46	0·91	−0·45
	4	3·600	0·0038	0·42	5·77	5·35	2·82	2·53
1932	1	3·558	−0·0117	−1·32	4·46	5·78	2·70	3·08
	2	3·655	−0·0188	−2·06	1·66	3·72	1·07	2·65
	3	3·478	−0·0058	−0·67	0·80	1·47	0·75	0·72
	4	3·273	−0·0046	−0·56	0·85	1·41	0·49	0·92
		London–Paris						
		Fr.	Fr.	%	%	%	%	%
1931	1	124·04	0·188	0·61	2·44	1·83	1·74	0·09
	2	124·26	0·287	0·92	2·33	1·41	1·27	0·14
	3	123·91	0·413	1·33	3·58	2·25	1·40	0·85
	4	91·87	0·403	1·76	5·77	4·01	1·82	2·19
1932	1	90·54	0·123	0·54	4·46	3·92	1·77	2·15
	2	92·77	0·043	0·18	1·66	1·48	1·53	−0·05
	3	88·77	−0·022	−0·10	0·80	0·90	1·00	−0·10
	4	83·56	0·002	0·01	0·85	0·84	0·97	−0·13

In the absence of special measures, this gap would have disappeared automatically through the purchase of foreign exchange discussed above. The sellers of foreign exchange would have received a cheque drawn on the Bank of England, and the cash reserves of the clearing banks would have been *pro tanto* enlarged. Chart I indicates that in the early months of 1932 this expansion of the credit base was not allowed to occur. When the Bank purchased foreign exchange 'other securities' in the

[1] Source: Einzig, op. cit., Appx. I. Averages are those of the mean quotation of the last week in each month.
[2] Source: Ibid., Appx. III.

Issue Department rose, and – since the fiduciary issue was fixed – an equal and opposite movement took place in the Issue Department's 'government securities'; these would have been transferred to the Banking Department in exchange for the foreign currency. If no other action had been taken, this would have amounted to open market operations on the part of the Banking Department, since both securities and deposits would have increased; to neutralize the process, the Bank would have needed to sell securities, restoring deposits and securities to their previous level. With the reservation mentioned above, interest rates would have been unchanged.

The Bank returns suggest, however, that during January and February of 1932 the Bank was selling securities when this neutralizing process would have required purchases to offset sales of foreign exchange by the Issue Department.[1] The fall in interest rates during this period was therefore occurring despite the Bank's actions, not at all because of them. From March onwards, however, a distinct change is noticeable. This change is such that it cannot be explained by purely seasonal factors. In Table V below, the movements in the Banking

TABLE V. PERCENTAGE CHANGES IN SECURITY
HOLDINGS OF THE BANKING DEPARTMENT

	1931	*1932*	*1933*
January–February	− 27·7	− 31·6	+ 3·5
March	− 4·2	+ 22·3	− 18·9
April–May	− 3·7	+ 7·4	− 8·6

Department's security holdings in the early months of 1932 are compared with those in the similar months of the preceding and following years. It will be seen that the decline during January and February of 1932 was distinctly greater than usual at this time of year, while from March to June the changes were actually contra-seasonal. Between March and June of 1932, the Banking Department's holdings of securities rose some £37 million; securities transferred from the Issue Department amounted to £44 million. Over the four months, therefore,

[1] Probably to the Treasury for the purposes of its credit repayment early in March

only around £7 million of the foreign exchange purchases had been neutralized; the remainder had been allowed to serve the function of open market operations. With the exception of the weeks 9–16 March and 6–20 April, the rise in security holdings was continuous. The two falls were associated with the Treasury's repayment of foreign credits, arrangements for which were announced on 9 March and 5 April respectively. Under the impact of these purchases, clearing bank deposits, which had fallen steadily between December 1931 and February 1932, rose from an average of £1,659 million in February to £1,764 million in June; the average rate on Treasury Bills fell from 4·00 per cent in February to 0·85 per cent in June, while the Consol rate fell from 4·50 to 3·89 per cent. The foreign exchange gap, as Table IV shows, disappeared. Bank rate was reduced from 6 per cent on 18 February to 3½ per cent by the end of March and 2 per cent at the end of June.

What is the explanation of this sudden change in tactics on the part of the authorities in March 1932? As has been noted above, the authorities were almost as anxious to prevent sterling appreciation early in 1932 as they had been to prevent depreciation in the preceding September. Why, then, had the Bank deliberately obstructed the fall in domestic interest rates by open market sales, and encouraged the persistence of the exchange gap which was one of the attractions of London for foreign funds? Why, in other words, did the Bank for the first two months of 1932 attempt to prevent the symptom – sterling appreciation – without taking the obvious step to remove one of the causes?

Some writers have concluded from this apparently illogical behaviour that official policy was nervous and confused. Mrs Hicks comments, 'In the spring of 1932 it seems to have been perceived rather suddenly that at any rate on monetary grounds a somewhat sharp reversal of policy was desirable.'[1] Other writers speak of a 'conversion to a cheap money policy'[2] or a 'reversal of policy'.[3]

[1] *Finance of the British Government*, XXIII, p. 363.

[2] Morton, op. cit., XIV, p. 244.

[3] Hallowell, op. cit., I, p. 7. Harris adumbrates mystification over the whole affair – *Exchange Depreciation*, XV, p. 410. Mr McKenna, surveying the Bank of England's policy in 1932, stated that 'in February a complete change of policy occurred' (speech at the Midland Bank A.G.M., 27 January, 1933).

This is surely a misconception. For the first quarter of 1932 the Bank of England was pursuing a perfectly consistent policy. It had two aims: (*a*) to acquire gold and foreign exchange with which to repay the American and French credits raised in August 1931; (*b*) to prevent the appreciation of the pound. Until the first requirement had been filled, therefore, the Bank wanted the best of both worlds. It did not want to check the influx of foreign exchange, but it also did not want the influx to have its normal effect on the rate of exchange. Its action, therefore, in maintaining the interest gap open and checking the appreciation of the pound by direct operation in the market was the only one open to it. By early March the bulk of the foreign credits had been repaid, and the remainder was repaid by the beginning of April. Of the Bank's credit of £50 million, £20 million had been repaid in October 1931, and the remaining £30 million in January 1932. Of the Treasury credit of £80 million, arrangements to repay £43 million were announced on 4 March, and the remainder on 29 March and 5 April. The major repayment, therefore, coincides exactly with the abandonment by the Bank of the policy of neutralizing the effect of foreign exchange purchases. It is similarly noticeable that immediately after the announcement of 4 March, restrictions on private foreign exchange purchases were withdrawn, while shortly afterwards South African gold supplies reappeared on the market. Previously, although such gold was flowing in at about the pre-September rate, it was not sold in the open market but to a 'special buyer', upon whose official identity all observers agree.[1] The credits repaid, the need to maintain the interest gap disappeared, and the reduction of interest rates, as well as direct operations in the exchange market by the Bank, and later the Exchange Account, were employed to check the unwanted appreciation of sterling.

The open market operations of the Bank were not, of course, reversed when the influx of funds became an efflux later in the year, and sterling began to approach, and fall below, its low December 1931 value of $3·372. By then the cheap money policy had been established in its own right, and the conversion of War Loan had been carried through. From being an offshoot of foreign exchange policy, cheap money advanced to a domi-

[1] See Brown, op. cit., ch. 31, pp. 1099–1100.

nant position among the aims of policy. But the original impetus for the credit expansion sprang from the desire of the authorities to prevent the appreciation of sterling in the face of an influx of foreign capital. Such, then, was the sequence: interest rates began to show their first downward tendency, limited and hesitant, as a result of the revival of confidence at home; official actions were at first opposed to, then combined with, this movement as an outcome of foreign exchange policy; finally, in mid-1932, the cheap money policy emerged in full force in its own right and for its own sake. Obviously, an overwhelming advantage of a cheap money policy was the alleviation of the debt burden it made possible; it was indeed a heaven-sent aid to achieving a balanced budget at a time when a balance was both difficult and a commitment of the government.[1] Later still, its usefulness in stimulating recovery attracted more attention. From a by-product, cheap money became a vital element in official policy.

[1] See Brown, op. cit., ch. 31, pp. 1131–2; Hicks, op. cit., XXIII, p. 361; Morton, op. cit., XIV, p. 243. The conversion of War Loan to a $3\frac{1}{2}$ per cent basis represented an annual net saving of £23 million.

4 The Return to Gold, 1925

R. S. SAYERS

[Written *c.* 1957, as a paper to be read to an audience in the University of Leeds, published as chapter 12 of L. S. Pressnell (ed.), *Studies in the Industrial Revolution*, London, 1960.]

Although its subject is a single brief episode, this paper is rather to be regarded as a plea for the systematic study of recent monetary history. I am pleading for a trade I have made my own, because its very nature causes it to be neglected, although it is of high importance to a full appreciation of problems of economic policy. To develop a taste for monetary history a student must have a pretty good grasp of monetary theory, and the expert in monetary theory is apt to succumb either to the fascination of highbrow theory or to the temptation to expend his energies in controversies about current policy; in either event he has no time for history. The historian, on the other hand, with plenty of other aspects of the past to study, is disinclined to get himself involved in a subject in which he fears the professional economists may easily catch him out. So monetary history falls between the stools.

What is the result? It is not that we have no monetary history at all, but that we have a lot of bogus monetary history, largely composed of the old skins thrown off by the snake of controversy. No matter how unhistorical they are, most people engaged in the controversies of economic policy do use arguments avowedly based on an interpretation of recent events, and this interpretation, being bandied about in current controversy, tends to harden into the accepted view of history. Yet it is most unlikely to be a sound view: it will have been based on the evidence of the moment alone, and its shape may well be influenced, if not dictated, by the more striking phrases of the controversialists.[1] One of the qualifications of the effective controversialist is ability to coin the striking phrase; these phrases

---

[1] This sentence stands as originally printed, though my careless use of the phrase 'a sound view' misled Professor Asa Briggs (*Econ. Jnl*, 1962, p. 197). I agree that all history is a matter of debate; all I meant was that we want our history to be firmly based on the ascertainable facts with due regard to their chronological order.

and the evidence of the moment form the basis of the view commonly taken of an episode as it slips back into the past. Though this process may be repugnant to the scholar, it would not greatly matter were it not that this accepted view itself becomes one of the arguments bandied about in the next phase of monetary controversy. The policies of tomorrow are influenced by today's slipshod history of yesterday; this is the evil we should seek to correct by turning our searchlights on to the recent past.

That completes the generalities that lie behind my view of an episode in recent monetary history. Through the remainder of this paper I shall be dealing with the restoration of the gold standard in 1925, because I believe that this episode provides a sharp illustration of the traps into which we may fall when we neglect the systematic study of monetary history.

The restoration of the gold standard in itself can be described very shortly. After being pegged by official dealings through the latter part of the war, at a rate close to the old parity, the dollar rate was allowed to slide from March 1919, and reached its low point of 3·20 in February 1920. The restoration of the gold standard, at a tacitly assumed rate of 4·86, was government policy throughout, and corrective measures for the low exchange were taken from the autumn of 1919 onwards. The wartime measures modifying the gold standard had been replaced in 1920 by the Gold and Silver Export Embargo Act. The term of this had been fixed at five years, ending 31 December, 1925. There was no special significance about this period (it is a common period for temporary legislation when one year is obviously too short); but when 1925 came round something had to be done about it. Policy in the intervening years had been directed, though not in an extreme way, to restoration of the gold standard, and in 1924 reasonably favourable conditions had helped the exchange towards par. A decision had then to be taken, and the decision was announced in the Budget Speech at the end of April 1925. The gold export embargo was effectively suspended forthwith, and the Gold Standard Act established a gold bullion system, the old parity of $4·86 to the £ being the basis.

The commonly accepted view of this step is that it was a grave mistake, made by Churchill after he had been misled by his official advisers; that the interests of British industry were, in some measure, sacrificed to the interests of the City of London as an international trading and financial centre; that it was a gamble on a rise in American prices that did not materialize; that the resulting international disequilibrium was the prime cause of the relative stagnation of the British economy through the second half of the twenties; that the resulting weakness of sterling was a major factor in the international currency collapse of 1931 and that the policy of 1925 was thus one of the remote causes of the cruel waste of the thirties. It is this view that has become part of the background of all recent argument on both short-term and long-term policy for sterling; it has given an air of historical justification to the case against any measures of exchange rigidity. I am going to suggest that, when all the evidence now available is reviewed, it is possible to interpret events quite differently.

But first I must say a few words about how the common view developed. It was by no means the immediate reaction of the commentators. *The Times* (29 April) claimed that the great majority of businessmen would rejoice in the return to gold. *The Economist* (2 May) expected it to effect 'a definite broadening of the base of British commerce'; the new policy was subject for congratulation to the Chancellor and was 'the crowning achievement' of Montagu Norman. The *Yorkshire Post* (2 May) and the *Manchester Guardian* (5 May) were equally comfortable. The President of the Federation of British Industries had much more to say about other (now forgotten) aspects of the Budget, but did find a moment in which to welcome the return to gold as a step towards a revival of foreign investment and the conquest of new markets. Criticism in the House of Commons had the empty ring of the formal duty of His Majesty's Opposition and was not pressed.[1]

During the summer of 1925 opinion began to change rapidly. Keynes wrote a series of articles in *The Nation* and the *Evening Standard*, and these were reprinted as a pamphlet with the stinging title *The Economic Consequences of Mr Churchill*;[2] Stamp lent his weighty support to Keynes's main thesis in his Adden-

---

[1] The Chief Opposition spokesman was Philip Snowden, who was in such matters always a pillar of 'orthodoxy'. The account given in his *Autobiography* (1934), ii, 721–2, was written in the light of later troubles and gives the impression of stronger doubts than were in fact voiced in 1925.

[2] Hogarth Press, (1925), (Essay 1).

D

dum to the Report of the Court of Inquiry concerning the Coal Industry Dispute.[1] Keynes treated the whole thing as a blunder; his explanation of why Churchill did 'such a silly thing' was that 'he was gravely misled by his experts'. Churchill's repentance gathered strength until he has almost come to believe that it was 'the greatest mistake of his life, and that he was bounced into it in his green and early days by an unholy conspiracy between the officials of the Treasury and the Bank of England.'[2] In fact it was an exceptionally well-considered step, Churchill's final decision only coming after a long series of official papers and, at the end, a dinner-party that was a kind of Brains Trust with opposing views voiced by the most eminent authorities. The argument of the case may be said to begin with the Cunliffe Report of 1918; after that date every government had proclaimed its intention of working towards the earliest possible restoration of the gold standard.[3] At the Genoa Conference in 1922 British delegates had taken the lead in advocating a universal return to gold, at previous parities where possible. The Bank Chairmen had pronounced in its favour (though not ignoring difficulties) and as lately as March 1925 the Federation of British Industries addressed to the Chancellor an Open Letter advocating restoration of the gold standard and not even referring to any disequilibrium in the international price situation.[4] The only real opposition came from a small group round Keynes, and there were critical noises in the Beaverbrook Press. The critics had their representatives in Churchill's private circles, and they worried him. Consequently, despite the overwhelming pressure of opinion in favour of restoration, the whole subject and all possible courses of action were thoroughly argued out

[1] *BPP*, 1924–5 (2478), xiii, 21–23.

[2] P. J. Grigg, *Prejudice and Judgment* (1948), p. 180. The following account of Churchill's consultations is based on Grigg's pages 180–6; Grigg was at the time in the Treasury and was the Chancellor's Principal Private Secretary.

[3] On the views of the Bank of England, see Sir Henry Clay, *Lord Norman* (1957), ch. iv.

[4] In view of this document, I find disingenuous the 'I-told-you-so' element in the evidence tendered by the F.B.I. to the Macmillan Committee in 1930. (Committee on Finance and Industry, *Minutes of Evidence*, i, 186–210.) This evidence included reproduction of the written evidence tendered by the F.B.I., July 1924, to the 'Bradbury Committee', urging delay and caution in the return to gold, but the Open Letter of March 1925 would seem to indicate that the F.B.I., like many others, came round to the policy of immediate return as conditions seemed in the winter of 1924–5 to become more propitious.

in official circles and put before the Chancellor both in written memoranda and in oral discussions. In these discussions there was no concealment of the pains of adjustment.

Finally Churchill gave a dinner party, Niemeyer and Brad-bury invited to represent the Ayes and McKenna and Keynes the Noes; Grigg was there as the Chancellor's Private Secretary, and it is from him that we have the story. Plenty was said about the risks of unemployment, falling wages, prolonged strikes and the contraction of some of the heavy industries. I suspect that Keynes was not at his most effective: he did not in those days carry his later weight, and he was always liable to have an 'off-day'. At any rate, Churchill was not completely convinced by Keynes's gloomy prognostications and turned to McKenna, who had wobbled somewhat in his latest public pronounce-ments. Churchill in effect asked McKenna: 'This is a political decision; you have been a politician, indeed you have been Chancellor of the Exchequer. If the decision were yours, what would it be?' McKenna, after wobbling to the end, replied, 'There's no escape; you have got to go back; but it will be hell.'[1]

So much for the story that Churchill was misled by his official advisers. I must now turn to two elements in the case that was made. First, there is the idea that the interests of British industry were sacrificed to the interests of the City of London: in effect, that Montagu Norman cared more for top hats in the City than for cloth caps in the streets of Lancashire and the valleys of South Wales. Nothing could be further from the truth, for the gold standard policy was essentially an employment policy. The post-war slump in Britain had reached bottom in 1922, and the slow revival thereafter had halved unemployment in the next two years, bringing it to around a million in 1924. At that level, or a little higher, it got stuck, and it was clear that Britain had an unemployment problem going beyond anything that could be explained by reference to the trade cycle. Analysis of the unemployment total revealed that the bulk of the remaining unemployment was in a few great export industries: coal, textiles, iron and steel, shipbuilding, which had been the staples in the terrific expansion of British exports in the genera-

[1] This is reported by Grigg as the substance of Churchill's question and McKenna's reply: naturally no verbatim record was made of the discussion.

tion before 1914. By the beginning of 1925 informed opinion therefore regarded the abnormal unemployment as a symptom of the difficulties of the staple export trades. Why were the export trades depressed?

This question, greatly debated up and down the country, was systematically tackled in the winter of 1924–5 by the Balfour Committee on Industry and Trade, a Committee predominantly of industrialists and traders, appointed by the MacDonald Labour Government in 1924. Its most important conclusions were published in mid-1925, after the actual return to gold, but the operative document is dated 12 March[1] and represents the views of intelligent businessmen during that winter when the gold standard policy was under consideration. The Board of Trade had provided the Committee with statistics showing that the proportion of British exports to total world exports had, if anything, risen since pre-war; the decline in Britain's export industries therefore appeared as an effect of causes operating not peculiarly upon Britain but upon the whole volume of world trade. For this general decline in world trade, the Committee found two sets of causes, one temporary and the other more permanent. The permanent cause was the growth of local manufacturers; this was a tough one, to be countered only by continuing inventiveness in the most advanced products and, as it was then argued, by 'rationalization' of the old industries.[2] Temporarily there was the dislocation of markets by wartime conditions; prominent among this set of causes was 'financial dislocation and the disorganization of currency and exchange'.[3]

The Committee itself did not there and then point the moral, but it was widely appreciated. Britain's unemployment problem was due to depression of world export markets; this was partly due to currency disorganization; therefore get the world's currency instability removed, the former foreign exchange stability restored, and export markets could be expected to revive and Britain's unemployment would dwindle. The world was waiting on the decision Britain had to take in

---

[1] It is printed as an Introduction to the *Survey of Overseas Markets* by the Committee on Industry and Trade (H.M.S.O., 1926).

[2] Cf. Clay, op. cit., especially pp. 166 and 356–7.

[3] The violent exchange fluctuations of the early 1920s had discouraged the export trades in much the same way as uncertainties of U.S. tariff policy operate today.

1925;[1] Britain's return to gold would give the lead and so give tremendous impetus to the movement towards international monetary stability.[2] A decision to return to gold at a lower parity would probably have had almost as good an effect. I must come back to this alternative in a moment; my immediate point is that the decision to go back to gold, far from being neglectful of the interests of British industry and the unemployed, was a decision calculated to eradicate one of the principal causes of trade depression and unemployment.

This viewpoint of business circles was urged upon Churchill by his advisers; that it was shared by competent outside observers is proved by *The Economist*'s immediate reaction to the announcement, which I have already quoted. And it did have its bearing on the question of adjustment to parity. Looking back, it is possible to suggest that the case for a return to gold appeared so overwhelming that insufficient attention was given to the question, 4·86 or 4·40? The Bradbury Committee did, it is true, brush this issue aside, partly on grounds of prestige.[3] Nevertheless, the question whether Britain could stand the 4·86 rate was looked into, at length, before the decision was taken. Churchill's advisers in general argued that there was still appreciable disequilibrium between British and American prices. The Bradbury Committee itself advised that a fall in the price level 'of a significant, though not very large, amount' was necessary,[4] and Keynes's own estimate of a 10 per cent gap was put before Churchill before he took his decision.[5] It is possible to argue that Churchill was not advised of the precariousness of all calculations of purchasing power parities; it was not until some time later that Gregory showed that quite a different answer to the sum resulted from choice of a more appropriate

[1] The Gold and Silver Export Embargo Act was due to expire at the end of the year.

[2] Cf. Clay, op. cit., pp. 141–2.

[3] To Montagu Norman no lower parity was acceptable, but he was willing to postpone return until 4·86 could be regarded as tenable (ibid., ch. iv). According to evidence given to the Macmillan Committee by the Federation of British Industries, the Federation had been told by the Treasury, apparently at an early stage in the Bradbury Committee's proceedings, that return at a 'devalued' rate was already ruled out of consideration (Committee on Finance and Industry, *Minutes of Evidence*, i, Q. 3188).

[4] *Report*, para. 19, reprinted in T. E. G. Gregory, *Select Statutes, Documents, and Reports relating to British Banking, 1832–1928* (2 Vols., 1929), ii, 376.

[5] Grigg, p. 182.

index number. However that may be, it is certainly not possible to say that Churchill was not warned of appreciable disequilibrium.

Nor is it possible to justify Keynes's assertion[1] that there was 'a gamble on a rise in gold prices abroad'. His assertion may have been based on a careless reading of the Bradbury Committee's paragraph 19, but their paragraph 22 showed that they assumed no better than 'stability' in America.[2] And in Grigg's report of the arguments used at the famous dinner party there is no mention of this among the points made by supporters of the gold policy. On the contrary, great stress was laid by Churchill's advisers on the risk that adjustment to the restored parity might be extremely painful.

Where I consider Churchill was ill-advised was in being led to suppose that the pre-1914 weapons of credit restriction were appropriate for bringing about the required adjustments. Keynes did make a point of this kind in his pamphlet,[3] but I should put it rather differently. In my view the ease of adjustments in Britain in the immediately pre-1914 period was based on the strength of London as an international lending centre, for this allowed London to shift much of the pain of adjustment on to other countries. Nothing like this was argued in 1925; I may perhaps be allowed to add that there had not been enough study of monetary history for people to appreciate the point.

I shall say no more about the arguments of 1925 but turn to the event. Churchill did decide to restore the gold standard, at the old parity of $4·86. By the time the Macmillan Committee reported in 1931 some of its members considered this act to have been a mistake, while others did not;[4] all agreed that it had 'required a reduction of sterling prices'.[5] The disequilibrium had been serious, perhaps of the order of 10 per cent: this was the general view, people differing only on the question whether the advantages of a gold standard policy had been worth the agony. As Keynes had predicted, internal costs proved decidedly resistant to any adjustment to the new parity, and the overvaluation persisted. The chronic difficulty of maintaining London's gold reserve and the international trade figures[6] support

---

[1] Op. cit., p. 12; and cf. his p. 27.
[2] Gregory, *Select Statutes, etc.*, ii, 376 and 377.   [3] Ibid., pp. 11 ff.
[4] *Report*, para. 242.   [5] Ibid., para. 113.   [6] Cf. below, pp. 94–5.

the view that there was this persistent overvaluation through the remainder of the twenties. There was certainly persistent depression in the old export trades, and continuing unemployment. McKenna's forecast that it would be hell proved all too correct; the hopes for an export revival to solve the unemployment problem proved illusory; and Keynes's criticism that 4·86 had posed too big an adjustment appeared to be all too well justified.

Nevertheless, I venture to doubt whether a choice of 4·40 as the 1925 parity, avoiding Keynes's 10 per cent adjustment, would have made much difference in any but the very short run. The initial strains were admittedly great, as most of Keynes's opponents had expected. But from the end of 1926 onwards international competition in the staple exports was gravely affected by the French and Belgian currency stabilizations, both at rates seriously undervaluing their currencies.[1] Now to anyone who reads the diary of Moreau, Governor of the Bank of France at the time, it is crystal clear that the French deliberately stabilized at a rate perpetuating the artificial advantage recently enjoyed by French export industries.[2] And what happened to the French franc had great influence on what was done about the Belgian franc. Hence a lower level of the pound would have meant an even lower level for the French and Belgian francs. Given the lack of international co-operation in these matters, this source of strain from 'exchange competition' in western Europe would have had to be faced by Britain whether the pound had been stabilized at one level or another. The trade statistics of various countries suggest that in fact the strain upon Britain came from Belgium rather than France. Between 1924 and 1927 Britain's share in world exports (by value) declined from 13 to 11 per cent; France's declined from 8 to 6·9, while Belgium's was maintained at 2·4 per cent. As sellers to Britain itself, France maintained her position with 5·2 per cent of Britain's imports, while Belgium's share in the market rose from 2·8 to 3·8 per cent.

[1] Cf. M. Norman's Evidence to the Committee on Finance and Industry (Macmillan Committee), especially QQ. 3355-62.

[2] E. Moreau, *Souvenirs d'un Gouverneur de la Banque de France* (Paris, 1954); pp. 177 and 182-3 are particularly relevant, and all Moreau's allusions to the subject show that France was not willing to face any dislocation consequent upon removal of the previous years' undervaluation of the franc.

The international trade figures of the period 1922–9 have a little further light to shed on the forces influencing international competition before and after Britain's return to gold.

TABLE A. VALUE OF MERCHANDISE EXPORTS
WORLD TOTAL, AND FOR SELECTED COUNTRIES
(*In U.S.A. gold dollars*)

Year	World exports $ million	U.K.	U.S.A.	France	Belgium	Germany
1924	27,185	3,538	4,498	2,169	644	1,559
1927	31,378	3,451	4,759	2,164	740	2,435
			Per cent of World Exports			
1924	100	13·0	16·5	8·0	2·4	5·7
1927	100	11·0	15·2	6·9	2·4	7·8

Source: League of Nations, *Review of World Trade*, 1936; *Memorandum on International Trade and Balances of Payments 1913–27* and *1927–9*.

TABLE B. VALUE OF UNITED KINGDOM IMPORTS
TOTAL, AND FOR SELECTED COUNTRIES OF ORIGIN
(*£ million*)

Year	Total U.K. imports £ million	Country of Origin			
		U.S.A.	France	Belgium	Germany
1913	768·7	141·7	46·4	23·4	80·4
1922	1,003·1	221·8	48·5	23·6	26·5
1924	1,277·4	241·2	66·6	36·4	36·9
1927	1,218·3	200·8	63·4	46·5	59·9
1929	1,220·8	196·0	56·5	44·0	68·8
		Per cent of Total U.K. Imports			
1913	100	18·4	6·0	3·0	10·5
1922	100	22·1	4·8	2·4	2·6
1924	100	18·9	5·2	2·8	2·9
1927	100	16·5	5·2	3·8	4·9
1929	100	16·1	4·6	3·6	5·6

Source: Annual Abstract of Statistics, U.K.

The U.K. was obviously losing ground relatively to all the other countries listed; Belgium was gaining ground relatively to the U.S.A., the U.K. and France; but the most striking feature is the resurgence of Germany as a competitor both in the U.K. market and in world markets generally. In fact, what was to happen again a generation later was happening in a milder form in 1924–9: the reconstruction of the German economy after the stabilization of the mark was a principal source of strain in international competition and upon sterling in particular. It was this resurgence of Germany, coupled with the deliberate undervaluation of the Belgian and French francs, that created for Britain a second problem of adjustment, and it was this second problem rather than the original act of overvaluation of sterling that made life such a misery for British exporters.

It is, of course, possible to argue that the choice of a more tolerable parity in 1925 would have allowed a margin, in the shape of a favourable balance of trade, which would have allowed Britain to take the later strains without catastrophe. To argue thus, it is necessary to argue that these later strains might reasonably have been foreseen. It is not reasonable to argue so in relation to the French and Belgian stabilizations. But the prevailing mentality behind Britain's decision in 1925 was a desire 'to get back to 1913', and indeed a belief that such a return was possible. A thoughtful and discriminating view of 'back to 1913' should have allowed for the possibility that Germany would win back something of her former trading strength. The superficiality of economic thought in high quarters passed over all such possibilities.

There is thus no doubt that, whatever the degree of blindness of responsible British authorities, the amount of adjustment required in the British economy was greater than had been foreseen. The later twenties did, however, show a quite considerable measure of adjustability in the British economy. Transfer of labour from one industry to another took place on a considerable scale. Although the volume of British exports still failed to reach the 1913 level, twelve out of the twenty groups into which the figures were divided showed that they had surpassed the 1913 level; these twelve included iron and steel and manufactures thereof.[1] By 1929 it was not fantastic to argue that the restoration of international currency stability had promoted the growth of world trade, that Britain had

---

[1] See Macmillan Committee, *Report*, Addendum III (T. E. Gregory), p. 223, and G. W. Daniels, 'Recent Changes in the Overseas Trade of the United Kingdom', *Transactions of the Manchester Statistical Society*, (November, 1930).

adjusted herself in part to the price disequilibrium created in 1925 even though that disequilibrium had been aggravated by the French and Belgian stabilizations, and that on a long view the 1925 action, taken by itself, had been worth while. There was still, of course, the major problem of excess capacity in certain of the old export industries, but the need for some fundamental reshaping of the British economy had been foreseen by Churchill's advisers in 1925 and had been represented by them, in my view correctly, as something that had to be faced anyway as industrialization proceeded elsewhere in the world.[1]

Then came the Wall Street slump. The immediate effect was to ease Britain's monetary problems. Very high rates of interest in America had been drawing short-term funds across the Atlantic, on an uncomfortable scale, and the easing of the tension in money markets brought a much-needed relief to the U.K. balance of payments at the end of 1929. The more fundamental effects of the slump came only in 1930, when it became clear that the movement was no mere Stock Exchange phenomenon. Precisely what these effects were on the British balance of payments we cannot say, because it was not until Britain ran into much more serious and more chronic difficulties that our authorities ever produced usable balance of payments statistics. But what evidence there is for the 1929–32 episode indicates that the balance of payments for the U.K. itself stood up remarkably well to the crisis: the steep relative fall in the prices of primary products, one of the extreme features of this slump, gave appreciable compensation for the contraction of the world's demand for U.K. products.[2] The balance of payments for the

[1] See the case put by Bradbury, as reported by Grigg, op. cit., p. 182. Sir Henry Clay, in his *Lord Norman*, which appeared after this paper was written, took substantially the same view.

[2] A comparison of the 1930 with the 1929 figures shows that, despite a decline of £182 million in visible exports, the net balance on income account deteriorated by only £76 million and this was compensated to the extent of £11 million by a decline in long-term lending. The figures for 1931 show the effect of the slump more fully, but are distorted by the events (including anticipation of imports to avoid intended import duties) of the latter half of the year. It seems likely that the continued heavy decline in invisible net receipts had already created a net adverse balance on income account in the first half of 1931, though this balance could quite easily have been compensated by the continued decline in long-term lending. All the available figures are assembled in convenient form by T. C. Chang, *Cyclical Movements in the Balance of Payments* (1951), table inset to face p. 144; and pt. ii of this book is the best available discussion of these facts.

sterling area as a whole must, however, have fared much worse; the peculiar relief to Britain as an importer had its counterpart in falling values of the exports of the Rest-of-the-Sterling-Area not only to Britain itself but also to the non-sterling countries. As the centre of the Sterling Area London therefore found that the relief from the Wall Street crash all too soon gave way to persistent weakness in the reserve position. Even so, 1930 was survived, and at the beginning of May 1931 the Bank of England still felt strong enough to participate in a concerted international move to reduce interest rates. But that did prove the last flicker of London's strength: the international liquidity crisis, which was nothing to do with London's monetary policy, was already bursting upon Central Europe and London's financial involvement in Central Europe ensured a quick spread of the crisis to London; and it was the development of this movement that broke London's attempt to maintain the gold standard. It is true that London's ability to withstand the crisis was undermined by continuing (and justified) talk of the over-valuation of sterling; but it is very difficult to believe that London would not have succumbed whether there had been over-valuation or not, especially when account is taken of the fact that there was an extreme American banking crisis just round the corner.

Thus, looking back I find it difficult to argue with any assurance that the 1931 collapse of the gold standard – and all that followed – was in any appreciable degree due to the over-valuation of sterling in 1925. If Churchill had accepted the 4·40 argument, we should still have had chronic depression in certain export trades, we should still have had the world slump and the international liquidity crisis, we should still have had the miseries of the thirties. It was basically the American trade cycle, and not British monetary policy, that made life so wretched for us.

My inclination is therefore to say that on the question of the valuation of sterling Churchill was fully advised, that the choice was made with substantial realization of the difficulties implied, and that the policy adopted was not substantially responsible for the major troubles of the next ten years. But that all refers to the *short-term* issue of the maladjustment in the international price situation. There was another issue, a long-term issue, that was not properly canvassed in 1925. This was the question whether London could, as a long-term policy, maintain a gold standard. (Keynes did just touch on it, but the question was generally neglected in controversy.) London's failure to maintain the gold standard in 1931 had no precedent before 1914 not because of the over-valuation but because of the fundamental change in London's position as an international financial centre. Before 1914 London had been able to survive the crises that followed each trade cycle explosion by pushing the main burden of adjustment on to other countries; since the First World War it has not been strong enough to do this, and when a veritable cyclone came in 1931 it was inevitable that the international gold standard should break down. It was this long-term risk, rather than the short-term risk of maladjustment, that was not taken properly into account in 1925.

And the reason for this omission is quite simple. In the years between 1918 and 1925 people had too often said that London's financial strength before 1914 was due to the gold standard. The truth was rather that the strength of the gold standard was due to London's international financial position. A little more systematic study of monetary history might have been useful in 1925, as well as now. I do not imply that a proper consideration of this point would have led to a different choice, nor that a different policy would have been better. The case for exchange stability for sterling in 1925 was very strong. But I do suggest that a fuller understanding of the past would have led to a proper appreciation of the long-term as well as the short-term risks, and more moderate hopes would at least have checked the revulsion against the gold standard, a revulsion that inhibited any reasonable degree of international monetary co-operation in the thirties.

5 The Reduction of Unemployment as a Problem of Public Policy, 1920–1929[1]

K. J. HANCOCK

[This article was first published in the *Economic History Review*, 2nd series, Vol. XV (December 1962).]

I

The chronic unemployment caused by the collapse of Britain's basic export industries in the twenties was inevitably an important political issue. The development of a social conscience before 1914, the growing acceptance of state intervention in economic affairs, the application of more sophisticated techniques for detecting social distress and the resounding pledges given by wartime statesmen about post-war conditions made it impossible for the state to be indifferent. At the general elections of 1922, 1923, 1924 and 1929 unemployment was a prominent question, and on each occasion the record of the retiring government was under criticism. The purpose of this article is to examine the policies adopted with the intention of reducing unemployment and to explain the failure of governments, in spite of these pressures, to adopt more adequate measures. Although the prevailing deficiencies of economic science were a major limitation, the policies and attitudes of governments require separate attention, because the difficulties emphasized by the politicians differed somewhat from those forming the agenda of learned debate. Unfortunately it is necessary to confine the article to the policies calculated to alter the level of unemployment and generally to ignore, except as an item affecting the budgetary position, the sustenance provided under the Unemployment Insurance Scheme.[2]

[1] In preparing this paper the writer was assisted by the comments of Profs. E. H. Phelps Brown and R. S. Sayers, of the London School of Economics, and Messrs W. F. Mandle and D. H. Whitehead, of the University of Adelaide.

[2] It is also necessary to ignore the rudimentary measures of protection and export promotion which were sometimes defended as employment-promoting.

The Government's views about the causes and likely duration of unemployment naturally affected the scope of its measures. Between 1920 and 1923 it was usual to attribute unemployment to the political and economic chaos in Europe and the consequent disruption of trade, and to insist that Britain could not prosper in the absence of European recovery. 'That', said Lloyd George, 'does not depend on Governments.'[1] Opening Parliament in 1922, the King stated that

> the great and continued volume of unemployment among my people causes me the deepest concern and will continue to receive the earnest attention of my Ministers. The only remedy for this distressing situation is to be found in the appeasement of international rivalries and suspicion and in the improvement of conditions under which trade is carried on all over the world.[2]

Throughout these years an early revival of trade was anticipated, and the measures adopted were correspondingly temporary. On the assumption that unemployment would largely disappear after the ensuing winter, the Government was expected at some time between August and October to announce a temporary programme of relief work. A valuable description of the official approach in these years was given in 1925 by Sir Alfred Mond (later Lord Melchett), Minister of Health in the Coalition Government. Referring to a speech by Sir Arthur Steel-Maitland, the Minister of Labour, Mond commented that:

> he seems to be still in the atmosphere of the period which I remember so well, when I was chairman of a Cabinet Unemployment Committee, and when the orthodox view seemed to be that you were still dealing with a state of things in which unemployment went up automatically in the autumn and came down automatically in the summer; that if you could devise some scheme to get over the trouble from October to March or April, you were dealing with the problem; and if you proposed any scheme which lasted longer than six months, you were gravely informed that it

[1] *Parliamentary Debates* (subsequently referred to as *P.D.*), (1921) 147, column 194.
[2] *P.D.* (1922) 150, col. 345.

was a very unwise thing to do, because probably by the end of that time there would be no more unemployment. That delusion has been going on for three or four years. Had the great schemes which were outlined three or four years ago been started, they would today be in operation. I remember an important scheme for building a canal from the Forth to the Clyde which was turned down on the ground that by the time it was finished there would be no unemployed. That was three years ago. That scheme would almost be completed today. It would have employed 100,000 men.[1]

The French occupation of the Ruhr in 1923 destroyed all hope of an early trade revival. It was this event which ostensibly led Baldwin to seek a mandate for protection as a long-term remedy for unemployment. 'A change came over the whole situation during the present year', he said, in defending his decision to recommend a dissolution. 'I think we must all of us be convinced that, owing primarily to the occupation of the Ruhr, and the effect which that has had on the economic position of Germany, the restoration of Europe has been postponed for years.'[2] The electorate was evidently unimpressed by Baldwin's proposals, and the Labour Government resumed the quest for European recovery by seeking a *modus vivendi* with Russia and by endeavouring to expedite the negotiations which produced the Dawes Plan.[3]

It was the rapid deterioration of the coal trade, beginning in 1924, which precipitated a decisive re-assessment of the relationship between world conditions and Britain's unemployment. The new Baldwin Government, precluded by an electoral pledge from moving towards general protection, acquiesced at first in the old assumption that European revival was a precondition of British prosperity. During the 1925 coal crisis, however, Baldwin realized that the occupation of the Ruhr, which in 1923 had been regarded as the obstacle to revival, had in fact moderated the depression by affording to the coal industry a respite from continental competition.[4] By 1925 the stabilization of European relations was within reach, but the return to prosperity in Britain seemed more remote than ever.

[1] *P.D.* (1924–5) 182, col. 780.   [2] *P.D.* (1923) 168, col. 117.
[3] See the speech by the Minister of Labour, *P.D.* (1924) 170, col. 2005.
[4] *P.D.* (1925) 185, col. 2071.

Because of its pre-occupation with industrial disputes, the Government was slow to implement the revisions of policy which this reassessment implied. For some months the stoppages were undoubtedly responsible for much unemployment, and subsequently they provided a politically convenient excuse.[1] By the end of 1927, however, it was firmly accepted that several of the great export industries had permanently lost a large proportion of their traditional markets. The necessity of modifying the industrial structure of the work force was accordingly recognized, and this recognition was directly responsible for the inauguration of the Industrial Transference Scheme.

II

The development of counter-cyclical policies entailing Government expenditure was inhibited by the prevailing budgetary and monetary policies. The principal budgetary objectives were to curtail expenditure and to reduce the National Debt. Some indication of the success of this policy is given by the accompanying table. The aggregates which it contains are adaptations of those to be found in the Budget papers and it is hoped that in a national accounting sense they are more useful. In the case of expenditure the largest items of a purely transfer nature, namely, those relating to the service of the National Debt, are excluded; while the surpluses include the contributions, if any, to the National Debt Sinking Fund. The composite price index by which the money aggregates are deflated is naturally very crude, but some allowance must be made for the price changes which occurred during these years. The table reveals the inability of governments to revert to pre-war levels of expenditure, in spite of their anxiety to do so; but it also indicates the deflationary significance of the rapid curtailment of Government demand after 1920. It is the size of the surpluses, however, which most definitely underlines the importance of the policy of debt retirement.

The only Chancellor to countenance any serious departure from the policy of debt reduction was Sir Robert Horne, who in his 1922 Budget proposed to suspend debt repayment in

---

[1] As late as November 1928 Churchill said that 'all of us . . . are suffering from the consequences of 1926, and the price has to be paid. The one supreme, definite, obvious, recent cause of the delay in the general trade revival lies there. We warned you of these consequences beforehand.' *P.D.* (1928–9) 222, col. 258.

IMPORTANT AGGREGATES OF GOVERNMENT FINANCE[1]
1913–14 AND 1919–20 TO 1928–29 (£ m.)

Financial year	Expenditure (other than on National Debt)	Net realized surplus	Composite price index	Expenditure at 1913–14 prices	Surplus at 1913–14 prices
1913–14	177	6	100·0	177	6
1919–20	1,329	—326	239·7	554	—136
1920–21	851	238	277·1	308	86
1921–22	755	55	225·6	335	24
1922–23	596	102	185·7	321	55
1923–24	450	88	177·5	254	50
1924–25	459	49	183·0	251	27
1925–26	480	36	180·2	266	20
1926–27	474	23	178·6	265	13
1927–28	470	69	175·6	268	39
1928–29	460	76	174·1	264	44

order to reduce taxation – a proposal suspected of political motives because of the imminence of a general election.[2] In his relatively flexible attitude to debt retirement Horne seems to have enjoyed some support from Bonar Law, whom he occasionally quoted:

I remember Mr Bonar Law saying in this House that what we ought to aim at was to pay off large sums of debt when we have a good year and to pay off smaller sums in a bad year. Obviously that is the principle which any business man would follow.[3]

[1] The undeflated aggregates are calculated from *Statistical Abstract of the United Kingdom 1913 and 1916–29*, Parl. Papers 1930–1 (Cmd. 3767), XXIX, pp. 121–7. Expenditure comprises the item 'Total expenditure chargeable against revenue', plus 'Total issues to meet capital expenditure', less 'Total National Debt services'. The price index combines a wage index with the cost of living index and *The Statist's* Wholesale Price Index, the weights being one-half, one-quarter and one-quarter respectively. The wage index is calculated, for the years 1925–6 to 1928–9, from A. L. Bowley, 'A New Index-number of Wages', published as Special Memorandum no. 28 of the London and Cambridge Economic Service. For earlier years it is calculated from various numbers of the Service's *Monthly Bulletin*, the figures thereby obtained being multiplied by 1·089 in accordance with Bowley's estimate of the degree to which actual wage increases were understated by December 1924. Since the discrepancy was probably less in earlier years, the index may slightly overstate the inflation between 1913–4 and the early 1920s. The cost of living index is obtained from the above *Statistical Abstract* (p. 107) and the Wholesale Price Index from various numbers of *The Statist*.
[2] In the event an unanticipated surplus allowed debt repayment to be continued.
[3] *P.D.* (1927) 205, col. 392.

Evidently Stanley Baldwin, as Bonar Law's Chancellor in 1923, was unimpressed by his leader's businesslike principles. Indeed, all Chancellors in the twenties other than Horne – Austen Chamberlain, Stanley Baldwin, Philip Snowden and Winston Churchill – were slaves to the debt. Not all, of course, achieved the reductions which they desired; in particular, Churchill's heroic programme of debt retirement was undermined both by the coal subvention of 1925–6 and by the financial consequences of the 1926 disputes. But the significance attached by Churchill to the appearance of debt reduction is exemplified by the dubious expedients that he employed to maintain it, the most important being the transfer of a portion of the Road Fund (the accumulated proceeds of motor-vehicle taxation) to general revenue and the progressive curtailment of the period allowed to brewers for the payment of excise. 'It will be quite impossible', said Churchill in his 1927 Budget Speech, 'to repeat in another year or in other directions the processes which have been adopted this year. Every conceivable expedient has been considered and I am at the end of my adventitious resources.'[1]

The Government's alarm, acknowledged in the 1921 Budget Speech,[2] at continued high levels of expenditure in spite of declining revenues resulted in the appointment of a strong committee under Sir Eric Geddes, formerly Minister of Transport, 'to make recommendations to the Chancellor of the Exchequer for effecting forthwith all possible reductions in the National Expenditure on Supply Services, having regard especially to the present and prospective position of the revenue'.[3] Questions of policy were reserved for Cabinet consideration, although the Committee might indicate the economies which changes of policy would permit; but in the opinion of Hilton Young, Financial Secretary of the Treasury under Sir Robert Horne, the Geddes Committee was allowed to operate 'at the price, practically, of dethroning the Government of the day. The Geddes Committee practically became the Cabinet at that time.'[4] During the reign of the Geddes Axe, as it was called, parsimony was enshrined as a leading principle of government.

---

[1] Ibid. col. 99.   [2] *P.D.* (1921) 141, col. 78.
[3] *First Interim Report of the Committee on National Expenditure*, P.P. (1922) (Cmd. 1581), IX, p. 2.
[4] *P.D.* (1927) 205, col. 247.

The Committee's recommendations included further transference of burdens from the central Government to the local authorities; the cessation of school admissions before the age of six; a reduction of teaching staffs sufficient to raise the national average of 32·4 children per teacher in elementary schools to 50; the curtailment of scholarships for secondary education; the termination of training facilities for physically fit ex-servicemen; and the abolition of the Department of Overseas Trade and the Ministry of Transport – a suggestion justifying confidence in the chairman as a poacher turned gamekeeper.[1]

Some of the Geddes Committee's proposals were politically unreal, but every Chancellor accepted its cheeseparing approach. In Philip Snowden's words 'the function of the Chancellor of the Exchequer . . . is to resist all demands for expenditure made by his colleagues, and when he can no longer resist to limit the concession to the barest point of acceptance.'[2] In addition to numerous economies effected by the various departments, a parliamentary dose was administered by Churchill in 1926 in the Economy (Miscellaneous Provisions) Act, the main provisions of which were designed to reduce Treasury contributions to health insurance and to the Unemployment Insurance Fund.[3] The prevailing enthusiasm for economy very largely explains why the expenditure on relief works, which seems now to have been quite inadequate, appeared to contemporaries to be unsuccessful in spite of its being substantial. Chancellors were impressed not by the comparison between the cost of works proposals and the total level of Government expenditure, but by the comparison between the outlay on works and the precarious margin available for debt reduction.

Criticism of governments for their pre-occupation with budget surpluses should be tempered by recognition of the constraints imposed by the accepted monetary policy. In the absence of borrowing at the Bank of England, public borrowing, or failure to repay loans, might have entailed higher interest rates and would have produced distributive effects of debatable

---

[1] *First Interim Report*, op. cit. pp. 105, 109, 110, 116 and 148; *Second Interim Report*, P.P. (1922) (Cmd 1589), IX, pp. 15, 25.
[2] P.D. (1924) 176, cols. 2091–2.
[3] 16 and 17 George V, cap. 15.

merit. The most important evil inflicted by the determination to restore the gold standard may well have been the limitations to which it subjected budgetary policy.

The direct effects upon employment of the monetary deflation initiated by the Cunliffe Committee and of the return to gold in 1925 cannot be assessed in this article. However, the controversial nature of later discussions of these policies necessitates some attempt to obtain a correct perspective of their place in contemporary politics. The prevailing monetary policy was neither controversial nor considered to be very intimately connected with unemployment. In a separate article the writer has pointed out that among the economists only three – Keynes, Hawtrey and Bellerby – were severely critical of the deflation, and only Keynes and Bellerby vigorously opposed the return to gold.[1] The political agreement was even more general. As an example may be mentioned a report prepared in 1920 by a Joint Committee on the Cost of Living representing the Labour Party, the Co-operative Union and various trade unions. The committee recommended that 'legislation should be passed without delay to regulate the conditions of issue of notes by fixing an absolute amount which the notes circulated without security must not exceed, this amount to be gradually and periodically reduced until the depreciation of the British currency in terms of gold disappears'. It demanded also that the Government cease entirely financing expenditure from bank credit and that the floating debt be either repaid or funded.[2] These recommendations were very similar to the Cunliffe Committee's and they summarize Labour's policy in the ensuing years. In August 1924, for example, one of MacDonald's ministers, William Graham, declared that the Government would welcome a 'sound and healthy deflation'.[3] Although the return to gold in April 1925 provoked an Opposition censure motion, the motion was carefully confined to the alleged precipitancy of the decision, and even this limited criticism was compromised by an article which Snowden had written for *The Observer* a few weeks earlier advocating that an early return

---

[1] 'Unemployment and the Economists in the 1920s', *Economica*, XXXVII (1960), 309.

[2] Trades Union Congress, *52nd Annual Report* (1920), p. 119.

[3] *Nation and Athenaeum*, (18 October, 1924) Supplement, p. 135.

to gold be made, even at some cost and risk. Indeed, the only important politician who in 1925 opposed both the return to gold and the associated deflation was Sir Alfred Mond.[1]

By 1928 some uneasiness about banking and monetary policy had developed, and in a memorandum prepared by the T.U.C. for the Mond–Turner discussions a full public inquiry was suggested.[2] To this proposal, adopted by the Joint Conference for the discussions, can perhaps be traced the establishment of the Macmillan Committee. There was no suggestion, however, that the gold standard might be abandoned, and at the 1929 election both the Labour Party and the Liberals reaffirmed their loyalty to it.[3] The most important political circumstance affecting monetary decisions in the twenties was a general ignorance and an absence of debate. As the Labour Party said of monetary policy in 1928:

> it was the subject of astonishingly little political discussion. Indeed, until its consequences became painfully manifest, criticism of it was almost wholly confined to a few experts who foresaw what was going to happen. . . . What was lacking was an informed Parliamentary and public opinion, and the attitude of mind which regards such an issue as this as a matter of vital public concern.[4]

III

Employment on public projects was the principal device, other than the Insurance Scheme, with which the Government sought to assist the unemployed. Special work was begun soon after the appearance of severe unemployment towards the end of 1920. An unofficial Cabinet Committee on Unemployment was established in August 1920 and in the following February, when the number of insured persons unemployed exceeded 1·4 million, the Minister of Labour (Dr T. J. Macnamara) was able to give details of a works programme employing about 73,000.[5]

[1] *P.D.* (1924–5) 183, col. 54.

[2] T.U.C. Statement on Unemployment (1/12/1928, typed), pp. 3, 11.

[3] The Labour Party, *Labour and the Nation* (revised edn.), Supplement on Banking and Currency Policy, no pagination; *We Can Conquer Unemployment: Mr Lloyd George's Pledge* (1929), p. 7.

[4] The Labour Party, op. cit.

[5] *P.D.* (1921) 138, cols. 120–3.

The programme included the construction of roads and sewers, the preparation of housing sites, the provision of civil work in government establishments previously producing munitions, the arrangement of short time in government establishments to spread the available employment, and the execution of decorations and repairs on government buildings in advance of previously determined schedules. In addition, a Treasury Committee, known as the Unemployment Grants Committee, had been constituted under the chairmanship of Viscount St Davids to allocate Treasury funds for the assistance of local authorities that were prepared to accelerate relatively labour-intensive projects.

The special expenditure undertaken between 1921 and 1929 was, in essence, an extension of this programme. Most of the outlay was on road construction and on the assistance of projects approved by the St Davids Committee, and in both cases the Exchequer met only part of the cost. In the case of road work, the balance was provided by the Road Board and the local authorities, although in 1927 Churchill made the first of his 'raids' on the Road Fund and the Board's assistance was curtailed. Work approved by the St Davids Committee was financed jointly by the Treasury and the local authorities. The estimated cost of the road construction approved for special assistance between 1921 and 1929 was approximately £50 million, and of the schemes assisted by the St Davids Committee about £115 million.[1] It was estimated that the work approved by the Committee up to June 1928 would directly provide employment amounting to 3,928,167 man-months.[2] This represents an average employment at any point of time of fewer than 44,000 persons, or less than 0·3 per cent of the work force and about 4 per cent of the unemployed; and these calculations suggest that the approved schemes and the special road construction together employed, on average, not more than 0·5 per cent of the work force. No precise information is available regarding incidental employment on the preparation of materials

---

[1] These figures are based upon a table in U. K. Hicks, *The Finance of British Government 1920–1936* (1938), p. 194. Mrs Hicks's figures slightly understate the work approved by the St Davids Committee as they do not include work approved in a year later than that in which the application was received.

[2] Unemployment Grants Committee, *Seventh (Interim) Report* (1928), p. 12. A small proportion of the work approved was not undertaken.

and other auxiliary services, but it was generally believed that the numbers indirectly and directly employed were about equal.[1] Having regard to this belief and to the small amount of work provided by miscellaneous projects outside the two main categories, the writer suggests that relief works and related services may have employed about one per cent of the work force. Although this estimate ignores the secondary effects of the expenditure on aggregate demand, it is clear that special works secured no more than a very modest increase in employment.

A consequence of the attempt to minimize central government expenditure by imposing part of the burden upon the local authorities was that the amount of work undertaken was sometimes limited by the local authorities' resources. For example, the Government's programme for the 1923–4 winter included the expenditure of £3 million on the Manchester–Liverpool road, but the inability of the local authorities to pay their share prevented the project from being implemented.[2] Somewhat later the Government asked local authorities to undertake relief works without Treasury assistance. The lack of realism which this suggestion entailed is illustrated by a letter sent to the Prime Minister in 1928 by the Manchester City Council. The letter was a reply to a circular from Baldwin appealing to employers to engage miners transferred from distressed areas under the Industrial Transference Scheme. The Council, which was not controlled by the Labour Party, stated that in the previous eight years it had spent £2¼ million on useful work for the unemployed, but had received from the Government only a little over £500,000, and its letter continued:

> The unemployment relief works in respect of which grants-in-aid have been received are now practically completed, but there are other schemes which have been prepared which are available to be put in hand at once if the Government will offer reasonable financial assistance. The City Council has

[1] See, for example, Unemployment Grants Committee, *Second Interim Report* (1923), Appendix, p. 14; and *Memoranda on Certain Proposals Relating to Unemployment*, P.P. 1928–9 (Cmd. 3331), XVI, p. 52.

[2] *P.D.* (1924) 170, col. 2063.

done its utmost to execute work in advance of normal requirements in order to benefit the unemployed, and failing further assistance, it can do no more at present in that direction.[1]

This method of economizing was entirely reprehensible. The areas containing most of the unemployed were predominantly poor and the financial difficulties of their local authorities were exacerbated by the cost of relieving poverty. To provide public amenities equivalent in standard to the national average would itself have required a rate above the average, and the provision of relief works required the rates to be raised yet further above those prevailing in the areas of low unemployment. Until the derating scheme came into effect, in the latter half of 1929, this system of public finance was a disincentive to the establishment of industries in the areas where they were most needed. For the year ended 31 March, 1929 the mean rate in the Administrative County of London, where average unemployment was low, was 8*s.* 6·3*d.* In the City itself the rate was 6*s.* 10·2*d.*, but in Poplar, where many unemployed congregated around the docks, it was 15*s.* 7·9*d.* Ratepayers in Sheffield paid 20*s.* 8*d.*, in Liverpool 15*s.* 3*d.*, in Bradford 14*s.* 2*d.*, and in Blackburn 15*s.* 4*d.* The highest rate charged by a County Borough was 29*s.* at Merthyr Tydfil, whose Labour Exchange consistently reported unemployment percentages exceeding 70.[2]

Reinforcing the impact of 'sound finance' on the works programmes was a growing scepticism about the ability of governments, through expenditure, to create employment. This scepticism was firmly impressed by the Treasury upon successive Chancellors and became known as 'the Treasury View'. It gave added weight to the Gladstonian tradition – still respected – that money left with the taxpayer fructified better than money in the hands of the state. Two rather contradictory formulations, both commonly accepted by the same persons, were current. One formulation was that public works programmes merely altered the time distribution of employment, providing jobs today at the expense of the future; the other that any employment provided on public projects must inevitably be

---

[1] Quoted by J. R. Clynes, *P.D.* (1928–9) 222, cols. 250–1.
[2] Ministry of Health, *Annual Local Taxation Returns: England and Wales, 1928–9* (1930), Part II, pp. 10–11, 60–3.

subtracted from employment available elsewhere. The former doctrine was especially prominent between 1920 and 1924. Indeed, the explicit function of the St Davids Committee at its inception was to encourage the local authorities to undertake work in advance of the existing schedules. In the circumstances it was a ludicrous policy, since it implied that assistance could be given to projects the need for which was relatively remote, while more urgent work was being curtailed, mainly because of the Geddes Axe, in the interests of economy. The grotesqueness of this situation generally escaped notice and the policy of accelerating work prevailed so long as there was any hope of imminent recovery.

This hope, as we have seen, was firmly discounted by the Government in 1925. Stealing work from the future appeared to be less justified when there could be no confidence that the future could afford to lose it. In March 1925 the Minister of Labour argued that electricity schemes alone were economically justifiable, and added that 'you pay for the other schemes, which are only palliatives or, as I said the other night, stimulants, at the cost of the patient's vitality when he gets over the crisis'.[1] By this time, furthermore, greater weight was being attached to the latter of the above doctrines, and it became accepted that 'if you use money for one object it is not available to be used for another, and that it is better for it to be used in industry for the employment of men in that industry for which they are naturally skilled and to which they are suited, than in relief schemes to which they are not suited.'[2]

The influence of both doctrines is apparent in a change of policy communicated to the local authorities by the St Davids Committee in December 1925. Before granting further assistance, the Committee must be satisfied that the works proposed would be at least five years in advance of normal requirements, and that the areas in which they were to be executed were suffering exceptional unemployment, defined as unemployment exceeding 10 per cent according to the unemployment insurance statistics.[3] The amount of work undertaken was consequently reduced, to the extent that the number of persons employed on

[1] *P.D.* (1924–5) 182, col. 711.
[2] Sir Arthur Steel-Maitland, March 1926. *P.D.* (1926) 191, col. 473.
[3] Unemployment Grants Committee, *Fifth (Interim) Report* (1926), p. 21.

approved projects fell from an average of about 57,000 between the beginning of 1921 and the end of June 1926 to an average of less than 7,000 during the next two years.[1] The contradictory arguments that public works increased employment in the present at the expense of the future, and that they secured no net increase at any time, continued to be vigorously expounded; for example, Churchill used both in criticizing Lloyd George's works proposals in 1929, and apparently no one noticed the contradiction.[2]

A further revision of policy occurred in 1928, following the inauguration of the Industrial Transference Scheme. The St Davids Committee offered special grants, more liberal than those previously available for approved schemes, to areas of low unemployment capable of absorbing transferees. At least 50 per cent of the men employed on any project approved under the terms of this offer must be transferees.[3] Among the schemes approved for assistance on this basis were a new Fish Dock at Grimsby, the extension of the West India Dock, a road to facilitate work on the Manchester Corporation's new reservoir at Haweswater, and a sewerage scheme for Southampton and the surrounding area.[4] The implicit justification for these schemes was, of course, the desirability of redistributing employment in favour of the transferees.

The rationale of the Treasury's antipathy to relief works in the twenties is a matter for conjecture. In the economic literature the doctrine that the level of employment is largely independent of the amount of Government expenditure is associated with the name of Hawtrey. It was a direct implication of Hawtrey's monetary theory that relief works were justified only if those who gained employment were considered more deserving than those who would allegedly lose it.[5] However, despite his position at the Treasury, Hawtrey was expressing his own views and not the Treasury's. In response to the proposal for an extension of public works contained in the Liberal Party's

---

[1] Calculated from figures in the *Fifth Report*, p. 15, and the *Seventh Report*, p. 12.

[2] *P.D.* (1928–9) 227, cols. 30, 53–4.

[3] Unemployment Grants Committee, *Eighth (Interim) Report* (1929), p. 11.

[4] Ibid. pp. 4–6.

[5] For an outline and discussion of the rather arbitrary assumptions of Hawtrey's theory, see the present writer's article, 'Unemployment and the Economists in the 1920s', op. cit., pp. 310–11.

programme at the 1929 general election, the Baldwin Government instructed various departments to prepare memoranda dealing with both its economic implications and its practicability.[1] In its memorandum the Treasury asserted very briefly the futility of relief works and concentrated on its contention that costs of production were 'at the root of the problem' – an unsatisfactory analysis because acceptance of this diagnosis does not necessarily preclude remedies of the kind proposed. The main attempt by the Treasury publicly to justify its thesis is to be found in the evidence of Sir Richard Hopkins to the Macmillan Committee in 1930.[2] Implicit in the Treasury analysis, as explained by Hopkins, was a wages fund view of employment: in the economy there was a certain quantity of accumulated funds available to be advanced to labour, and the most that could be achieved by employment-promoting schemes was to ensure that these funds were fully used in providing employment. Hopkins conceded that public works might achieve something in this direction, first, through the saving on the dole, secondly, by transferring funds out of foreign investment into Government loans used for providing employment at home, and, thirdly, by mobilizing funds which would otherwise remain idle. However, he doubted the existence to any substantial extent of economically justifiable schemes, by which he meant schemes yielding a return to the Government less than the market rate of interest by only a moderate amount as an allowance for the social benefit of lower unemployment. Investment in other schemes might so disturb business confidence that private investment would decline by more than the increase in the public sector.

Although it would be easy to criticize this argument in the light of more recent economic theory, it was clearly far more subtle than the reasoning with which the Treasury had been credited. 'I find', said Keynes towards the end of Hopkins's examination, 'that the Treasury view has been gravely misjudged.' We may wonder, however, to what extent Hopkins's evidence reflected Treasury thought during the twenties, and whether it was not very largely a product of the controversy

[1] *Memoranda on Certain Proposals Relating to Unemployment*, op. cit.
[2] *Minutes of Evidence Taken Before the Committee on Finance and Industry* (1931), Vol. II, especially pp. 18–24.

which Lloyd George's proposals had provoked and of the necessity to state a coherent case before the Macmillan Committee. The great discrepancy between the 1930 evidence and the dogmatic and naïve statements of Snowden, Churchill, Steel-Maitland and others who had the benefit of Treasury advice gives ground for doubt whether the Treasury had earlier been tendering advice of the 1930 standard.

IV

The Industrial Transference Scheme was the Government's response to the uneven geographical distribution of unemployment. This problem is perhaps the aspect of inter-war unemployment which has most significance for modern applied economics. Though Keynesian measures may eliminate a general deficiency of demand, they cannot be relied upon to produce employment opportunities in the industries and areas where labour can readily take advantage of them. When confronted with pockets of severe unemployment in an otherwise fully employed economy, the Government, unless it leaves the unemployed to their fate, must choose between creating generalized excess demand sufficient to obliterate the more persistent pockets, and promoting a better relationship between the workers and the employment opportunities. The latter objective may be pursued, theoretically, either by taking the jobs to the workers or by taking the workers to the jobs. The Industrial Transference Scheme was an attempt to take the workers to the jobs.

To some extent the stagnation of particular areas was redressed by a spontaneous movement of population, so that even those areas where employment grew rapidly enough to absorb the growing indigenous work force could not escape serious unemployment. Marked inequalities persisted, however, in the unemployment percentages of the various regions. By 1927, when the Government began to think more seriously about unemployment as a long-term reality, the greatest concentrations of unemployment were in the coal-mining areas, and the Transference Scheme was intended to help the miners, although the problems of some shipbuilding centres were almost as acute.

The hopes placed in transference were not confined to spreading the hardships of unemployment more evenly. There was a seriously held belief that it would reduce unemployment without greatly adding to the costs of government. The Scheme was foreshadowed by the Blanesburgh Committee on Unemployment Insurance, whose report, tendered in January 1927, contained the following passage:

> If the right arrangements can only be devised, useful work can be found for a very large population of capable and willing workers. Specialization is the root cause of much unemployment. . . . Some of us have been impressed by the difficulty which certain growing industries experience in meeting their labour requirements, even though there are unemployed men in other industries where their services are not likely again to be required, at any rate for a considerable time.[1]

It is fair to state that the impression formed by 'some of us' of labour scarcities in 'certain growing industries' was supported neither by the unemployment statistics, which revealed a substantial reserve army attached to every expanding industry, nor by the evidence given before the Committee. Indeed, the principal witness from the Ministry of Labour assured the Committee that the Exchanges were experiencing no difficulty in filling any vacancies notified to them.[2] The Committee recommended, to facilitate transference, that transferees 'should be willing and should be permitted to work for a few months at a wage somewhat less than the standard rate, in the assurance that by the end of that time they will become sufficiently experienced to be worth the full wage.'[3] Not surprisingly, the only consequence of this proposal was to discredit the Committee in Labour opinion.

The first effective measure to reduce the work force in the mines was an agreement, effective from 1 August, 1927, precluding the engagement of any worker over eighteen years of age who was not in the industry before April 1926. This agreement terminated an undesirable movement of labour which had

[1] *Report of the Unemployment Insurance Committee* (1927), p. 26.
[2] Unemployment Insurance Committee, *Minutes of Evidence* (1927), p. 3.
[3] *Report*, p. 26.

brought some 17,500 workers over eighteen into coal-mining between July 1926 and July 1927.[1] In December 1927 the Government established a network of Juvenile Unemployment Centres in distressed areas to encourage and assist boys to move. The number of boys transferred through the centres in the following twelve months was less than 2,000, and this meagre achievement was made possible only by a public appeal for funds, the proceeds being used to supplement the wages of boys who could not otherwise have afforded to live away from home.[2] These, however, were relatively minor aspects of the scheme. To devise more comprehensive measures the Government appointed a new committee, the Industrial Transference Board.[3]

Reporting in June 1928, the Board stated that the coal industry was confronted with a permanent labour surplus of at least 200,000. Without being given specific executive authority, the Board was expected not only to inquire, but also to facilitate transference. Consequently its report combined objective findings with passages intended to popularize transference, and the Board moved between the two functions with such agility that it is difficult to know whether, in judging its remarks, one is applying an appropriate standard. Arguing that transference would increase employment, it asserted that 'each man taken on is adding to a flowing stream, not driving another out of a space of fixed dimensions. At a time of relatively good trade such as is now being enjoyed in a number of areas in this country, many employers are prepared to make an effort to start a good man.'[4] This is essentially a statement that some workers have higher marginal productivity than others. As such it is very nearly a tautology, and is correspondingly devoid of empirical significance. The Board's conviction that employing transferred miners would be profitable to industry remained a matter of faith.

The Board arranged for advances to be made through the Employment Exchanges towards the expense of removal and

---

[1] *Report of the Industrial Transference Board*, P.P. (1928) (Cmd. 3156), X, p. 12.

[2] Ministry of Labour, *Memorandum on the Transfer of Juveniles from Distressed Mining Areas to Employment in Other Districts* (1928), p. 5.

[3] The Board's members were Sir Warren Fisher, Sir John Cadman and Sir David Shackleton.

[4] *Report*, op. cit. p. 19.

towards the maintenance of families while accommodation was being sought. The publication of its report was followed by the dispatch of a circular letter from the Prime Minister to some 150,000 employers. Alluding to past co-operation in respect of the King's National Roll for assisting disabled ex-servicemen, Baldwin appealed to the employers to provide work for 'men who are strong, able and willing to work and whose wound is in their spirit'.[1] He asked them to discuss the matter with officers of the local Exchanges, which were assigned quotas of transferees to be given preferential treatment in the allocation of jobs. To reduce the likelihood of co-operating employers' receiving unsatisfactory labour, the Ministry of Labour's Adult Training Centres provided short courses of instruction for transferees.[2]

By the end of 1929 about 42,000 men had been transferred.[3] Although this seems to be a worthwhile proportion of the 200,000 surplus estimated by the Industrial Transference Board, the Ministry of Labour believed that by the middle of 1929 the cream had been skimmed, and was very despondent about the future prospects of transference. The Board's faith in the employability of unemployed miners proved to be poorly founded, and

> it became evident in the early part of 1929, mainly through the increased extent to which transferred men were failing to retain their jobs, that there was a change in the quality of men coming forward for transfer. In the main, this was probably due to the fact that the remaining surplus of men available had been continuously unemployed for longer periods than those who had first taken advantage of the scheme.[4]

Late in 1929 the Ministry investigated some 40,000 miners under the age of 45 (the older men presenting a still more hopeless problem) who had been unemployed for at least three months and found that only 7,500 were available and readily suited for

[1] *Ministry of Labour Gazette*, (September 1928) p. 314.
[2] T. S. Chegwidden and G. Myrddin-Evans, *The Employment Exchange Service of Great Britain* (1934), p. 156.
[3] Calculated from *Report of the Ministry of Labour for the Year 1928*, P.P. (1928–9) (Cmd. 3333), VII, p. 17; and *Report of the Ministry of Labour for the Year 1929*, P.P. (1929–30) (Cmd. 3579), XV, p. 16.
[4] *Report of the Ministry of Labour for the Year 1929*, p. 17.

industrial employment.[1] Subsequently the further decline of employment in mining threw up more transferable men, but at any point of time the great majority of unemployed miners were an intractable problem. The principal defect of the Industrial Transference Scheme, which limits its relevance to future circumstances, was the lack of attention to the aggregate demand for labour. The miners were being transferred to areas where unemployment was far from negligible. In a buoyant economy much of the workers' reluctance to move and much of the employers' reluctance to engage them might have evaporated. In an environment of high employment, transference may be a realistic remedy for the problem of depressed areas but in the circumstances of the twenties it was calculated to produce frustration, disillusionment and hostility.

V

In earlier sections the limits to employment creation defined by financial and monetary orthodoxy were outlined. The subject of this concluding section is a basic political reason for the readiness of governments to accept those limits. On the whole the interests of the unemployed were inadequately represented. The parliamentary and electoral debates on unemployment are tiresome for their number and repetitiveness, and outside Parliament a great clamour was created by the National Unemployed Workers Movement. But there was a too general acceptance, by those on whom the unemployed depended for effective representation, of the policies and attitudes which precluded measures for substantially reducing unemployment.

The Labour Party's acquiescence in, even its enthusiasm for, the deflationary monetary policy has already been noticed. Budgetary orthodoxy was a characteristic which it acquired less readily. After the war, indeed, there was a strong conviction that expenditure could be adapted to stabilize employment, and in *Labour and the New Social Order*, the document containing its policy for post-war reconstruction, the Labour Party declared that:

> in a modern community it is one of the foremost obligations of the Government to find, for every willing worker, whether

[1] Ibid.

by hand or by brain, productive work at standard rates. . . .
It is now known that the Government can, if it chooses,
arrange the public works and the orders of the National
Departments and local authorities in such a way as to maintain the aggregate demand for labour in the whole kingdom
(including that of capitalist employers) approximately at a
uniform level from year to year; and it is therefore a primary
obligation of the Government to prevent any considerable
or widespread fluctuations in the total numbers employed in
times of good or bad trade.

Arguments to this effect remained influential in the Labour
Party until its term of office in 1924, especially in the period
between 1920 and 1922 when J. R. Clynes was Parliamentary
Leader. In 1921, for example, Clynes urged the Government
'to step in and organize the workers of the country in employment that will produce wealth instead of allowing them to
remain in an idle state at somebody else's expense'.[1] The
Party's support for an expanded works programme in these
years probably reflects the persuasiveness of Sidney Webb. In
1921 he was chairman of a committee demanding 'immediate
steps to maintain economic demand';[2] and in 1923, having
estimated that the existing relief works were assisting only 3
per cent of the unemployed, he advocated loan finance to
support a much larger programme. He carefully insisted, however, that the loans must be subscribed by genuine investors
and not through an expansion of bank credit – that would be
'inflation'; but loans not associated with any addition to the
money supply would permit the use of idle capacity without
any rise in prices.[3]

After the return of Ramsay MacDonald and Philip Snowden
to positions of importance in the Parliamentary Party after the
1922 general election, Labour's support for such remedies
rapidly declined. MacDonald and Snowden would countenance
no deviation from the principles of 'sound finance'. In 1923
MacDonald denounced a proposal to use the unexpected revenue
surplus for accelerated housing construction and insisted on its
use for debt reduction;[4] and Snowden described Sir Alfred

---

[1] *P.D.* (1921) 138, col. 115.   [2] *Unemployment: a Labour Policy* (1921), p. 9.
[3] *P.D.* (1923) 161, cols. 882–7.   [4] *P.D.* (1923) 162, col. 1742.

E

Mond, who advocated slower debt repayment in order to stimulate industrial recovery, as a 'charwoman economist', because he imagined that Englishmen could live by taking in each other's washing.[1] Snowden's budget in 1924 was rigorously orthodox and thenceforth the Labour Party generally ridiculed works proposals. In 1925 Snowden stated that 'the great part of the money which has been spent in relief works . . . has been from the economic view almost wholly wasted'.[2] Churchill was repeatedly criticized by Snowden for his failure to effect greater economies and to make larger Sinking Fund contributions; Snowden disapproved the coal subvention because of its budgetary consequences, and he condemned as inadequate the savings envisaged in the Economy Act 1926.[3] Lloyd George's platform for the 1929 election was described by the Labour Party as 'madcap finance'; it is ironic that in rejecting the Liberal proposals the Labour Party used the caption 'after two years – the deluge'.[4]

For the unemployed Labour's period of office in 1924 was probably unfortunate. The Labour Government's achievements in respect of unemployment may be accurately summarized as a relaxation of the conditions of unemployment benefit and a moderate increase in the amount of work which the St Davids Committee might assist. It was soon clear that the Government proposed no radical remedies. 'Does anybody think', asked the Minister of Labour, 'that we can produce schemes like rabbits out of our hat?'[5] In the debates on unemployment Sidney Webb, although President of the Board of Trade, was practically silent. The effect of Labour's inability to improve substantially upon the records of its opponents was to reduce the political pressure upon the next Government to provide remedies. As Baldwin said, he was 'quite profoundly grateful that the Labour Party have been in office, and for this reason: that they, no more than any other Government, have been able to produce a panacea that would remedy unemployment'.[6] The unemployed might have expected the Labour

[1] Ibid. col. 2105.   [2] *P.D.* (1924–5) 182, col. 694.

[3] *P.D.* (1927) 205, cols. 224 and 231.

[4] The Labour Party, *Labour's Reply to Lloyd George – How to Conquer Unemployment* (1929), p. 9.

[5] *P.D.* (1924) 170, col. 2003.

[6] S. M. Baldwin, *Peace and Goodwill in Industry* (1925), p. 35.

Party to regard their needs as more urgent than the financial and monetary objectives which had inhibited other Governments; but their case was allowed to go by default. It was the extensive political support obtained for those objectives, making the man who dissented appear to be a crank, which made them so potent as causes of suffering.

6 The Gold Standard and Deflation: Issues and Attitudes in the 1920s

L. J. HUME

[This article was first published in *Economica*, (August 1963).]

In their attempts to grapple with the past, historians are apt to stress landmarks or turning-points, events which stand out in important respects from others that accompanied or immediately preceded them. Such an approach has, no doubt, considerable value, but it also carries with it certain obvious dangers. I suggest that these dangers now confront us in currently held views about the place of Keynes's writings on monetary policy during the 1920s (especially *A Tract on Monetary Reform* and *The Economic Consequences of Mr Churchill*) in the thinking of the time. Recognition of the incisiveness of Keynes's argument, and of the wholehearted way in which he dissented from the orthodoxy of the Bank of England and the Cunliffe Committee, tends to conceal the existence of other currents of dissenting opinion which existed at the same time and to some of which his thinking was quite closely related.

As examples of currently held views about the attitudes to monetary policy that were influential during the early 1920s, and about the significance of Keynes's attacks on orthodoxy, I want to refer to passages from the writings of three authorities on the period. The first is to be found in Professor Ashworth's volume in the Methuen *Economic History of England*. Ashworth sums up the matter in these terms:

> In order to bring back the exchange rate to par it was necessary to lower the British price level relatively to the American as a means of decreasing Britain's international expenditure relatively to its earnings. Since the American price level began to fall rapidly in 1920, the reductions needed

in British prices were formidable indeed. To bring them about a drastic restriction of credit was applied, mainly by means of high interest rates, despite the adverse repercussions this must have on business activity and employment. *This restrictive policy continued even in the depths of the slump in 1921 and 1922, when every other consideration would have suggested the opposite policy. Such was the prestige of the gold standard, however, that hardly anyone of authority or influence questioned the rightness of the policy.* One of the few notable exceptions was J. M. Keynes . . .[1]

A similar judgement, which at the same time introduces some new issues, is expressed in a recent article by Professor E. V. Morgan. 'Looking back on the monetary history of the 1920s,' wrote Morgan, 'one of the most surprising features is the unanimity with which economists and bankers, politicians and businessmen accepted the desirability of a return to gold at pre-war parity. . . . The return to gold was welcomed by most of the business and commercial world, including the Federation of British Industries. Keynes was almost the only consistent critic.'[2]

Finally, this broad picture is both confirmed, and filled out a little more, in the late Sir Henry Clay's biography of Montagu Norman. Clay wrote:

The official policy [as recommended by the Cunliffe Committee] . . . was seldom challenged; when it was, as it was implicitly by a plea for a little inflation by a former Junior Minister in the summer of 1923, it was reaffirmed by the Prime Minister (Baldwin). . . . Criticism came not from Parliament or industry or trade, and hardly at all from the City; but economists whose special studies lay in the field of monetary economics began to have doubts, and presently to oppose the accepted policy. Those criticisms centred on two issues – the delay in reversing the deflationary pressure of a high Bank Rate, and the determination to restore the Gold

[1] W. Ashworth, *An Economic History of England, 1870–1939*, (1960), p. 387. [Italics not in the original text.]
[2] *The Economist*, (17 June, 1961) p. 1268.

Standard at the old parity with gold and the dollar. No one seems to have opposed returning to the Gold Standard as such, until years after the return had been made.[1]

Elsewhere Clay argued that on the publication of the Cunliffe Committee's report 'public opinion . . . assumed without argument that the aim of policy must be to restore the pre-war Gold Standard in essentials',[2] and that criticism of the adoption of the pre-war parity came almost entirely *after* the return to gold in 1925, although he did note two suggestions made in 1922 (one by Keynes) that it might be advantageous to adopt a lower rate.[3]

There is, of course, always room for differences of opinion about when it is appropriate to say (as we all do) that opinion is nearly unanimous, that a belief is generally held or that criticism is seldom voiced. But it seems to me that, even if we take full account of the qualifications in the statements quoted above, they need to be supplemented if they are not to convey a misleading impression of the actual course and range of opinion about monetary policy between the publication of the Cunliffe Committee's Interim Report in 1918 and the return to gold in 1925.

The truth is, I suggest, that during those years there was persistent criticism – a good deal of it coming from industry and some of it from the City – of the Cunliffe Report and of the approach which it had recommended and which formed the official policy of successive Governments from 1919 onwards. There was also if not a deep questioning of assumptions, at least a certain realignment of arguments on the part of some of those who remained committed to the Cunliffe approach. The criticism of orthodoxy may have been proportionately small but in absolute terms it was not inconsiderable. Keynes might, indeed, be more appropriately regarded as having been, before 1925, in the vanguard of a movement rather than as a voice in the wilderness.

On a more specific point, Morgan's reference to the Federation of British Industries seems to be rather misleading, partly

[1] H. Clay, *Lord Norman*, (1957), p. 139. Cf. pp. 135–6.
[2] Ibid., p. 112.
[3] Ibid., pp. 155–6.

because the welcome the Federation accorded to the restoration of the gold standard in 1925 was a highly qualified one, but, what is more important, because it was from 1918 to 1925 one of the principal 'carriers' of the minority opinion of which Keynes was the most effective spokesman.

THE ISSUES: THE GOLD STANDARD AND THE CUNLIFFE COMMITTEE

In the passages quoted above, we can identify five issues on which Keynes held views that might be classified as unorthodox: the value of the Cunliffe Report as a guide through the policy-maze of the 1920s; the desirability of the gold standard as a system of monetary regulation; the appropriateness of the pre-war parity for Britain in the mid-twenties; the propriety of attempting to eliminate the gap between British and foreign (especially American) prices by means of a restrictive monetary policy (deflation); and the wisdom of returning to the gold standard in the circumstances prevailing in the early part of 1925.

Looking back from our present vantage point, it is easy to see these issues as closely related or even as interdependent, and to suppose that there existed a simple choice between ortho-doxy and heterodoxy. In the twenties, however, matters did not appear in quite the same light. In order to understand the trends and currents in opinion, it is best to give up altogether the notion of a single monolithic position against which Keynes was contending, and to concentrate instead on the several issues.

Of the five points identified above, the desirability of the gold standard as a system of monetary regulation was the least sub-ject to disagreement. Outside Keynes's immediate circle, it was generally accepted that this was preferable to any available alternative system as a permanent basis for international trade, although this did not preclude dissatisfaction with some aspects of the system. In this context, Britain's return to gold was viewed (not without justification, as events showed) as a step towards re-establishment of the international gold standard which was valued for reasons that have been summed up by Professor Morgan in the article quoted above.

Again, before 1925, there were few outside Keynes's circle who were prepared to contemplate the devaluation of sterling. The idea that other countries might have to devalue on returning to gold was made thoroughly respectable by the Genoa Conference in 1922, which declared bluntly that for many countries a return to the old parity was no longer 'feasible' and that the first country with a seriously depleted currency which fixed a new gold parity 'would render a considerable service to Europe'. But the idea that this advice might be applicable to sterling was generally, and for the most part instinctively, rejected.[1] There were a few people who accepted *in principle* Keynes's attitude that the pre-war rate of exchange was not entitled to automatic preference, but yet found overwhelming in practice the arguments against moving to a new parity.

On these questions of principle, then, we can agree that Keynes was in a more or less isolated position. But it does not follow that on more specific questions he was equally isolated.

In the first place, not everyone found the Cunliffe Report a satisfactory document. It was, in some respects, a curiously limited document. It ignored or brushed aside issues and considerations that even before the war had seemed important, and its discussion of the steps to be taken to re-establish the gold standard was very thin and, as time went on, increasingly irrelevant. From the first there was some comment on its omissions, and a critical attitude soon developed.

Secondly, it is certainly not true that the use of a restrictive credit policy went almost unquestioned between 1920 and 1925. On the contrary, from 1920 onwards there was vigorous and widespread opposition to the use of deflation as a weapon to bring Britain back to the gold standard while there was serious unemployment and trade and industry were stagnating. The .critics were by no means confined to 'economists whose special studies lay in the field of monetary economics', but included bankers, industrialists and financial journalists. It is true that the critical voices were mainly muted or absent when matters came to a head early in 1925. But even at this stage Keynes was not alone in regretting the Government's decision. And among his allies was the Federation of British Industries.

[1] But not *invariably* rejected. Cf. the views of Rylands, pp. 140–1 below.

THE EMERGENCE OF HETERODOXY: REACTIONS TO THE CUNLIFFE REPORT

There is no doubt that when the Interim Report (Cd. 9182, 1918) of the Cunliffe Committee was first published, public opinion was, as Clay argued, on the whole favourable. The tone of much of the comment was summed up in *The Economist*'s headline 'Back to Sanity'.[1] But alongside the favourable opinions there were also some criticisms and reservations. Looking back a year or so later, the *Bankers' Magazine* (still the main periodical devoted to the discussion of banking issues) complained that in 'the City . . . destructive rather than constructive criticism was the order of the day'.[2] This was probably an exaggeration, but there was some truth in the judgement.

Perhaps the best guide to the City's reactions is to be found in an early analysis of the report in the *Bankers' Magazine* itself. There its broad recommendations were cordially welcomed. But two qualifications were added. It was conceded that some people felt that in the Committee's 'zeal for deflation there is apparently insufficient regard for the claims of legitimate borrowers after the war'. To this the *Bankers' Magazine* replied that 'we do not think for a moment that it was intended to be suggested by the report that there was to be any drastic curtailment of facilities to the manufacturer or the trader on the part of the banks', i.e. that the burden of deflation was to fall mainly on the Government sector. On other points 'of somewhat minor importance' the *Bankers' Magazine* agreed that there was room for criticism, because insufficient heed had been paid 'to those who maintained that in many directions the Bank Act of 1844 required material alterations'.[3] The last point was echoed in the City Notes of *The Times*, where it was noted that the report gave 'an emphatic negative to most of the proposals for reform to which an extensive backing [had] been found in the general discussion of the last two or three years.'[4]

The general discussion of the war and pre-war years had in fact produced criticisms of the existing financial system and

[1] *Economist*, (2 November, 1918), p. 618.
[2] *Bankers' Magazine*, Vol. 109 (1920), pp. 39–40.
[3] *Bankers' Magazine*, Vol. 106 (1918), pp. 523–4.
[4] *The Times*, (30 October, 1918).

proposals for reform, including demands for the amendment of the Bank Charter Act. These criticisms and proposals, to which the Cunliffe Committee made remarkably few concessions, provided the starting-point for the first critics of the Report.

The pre-war discussion had centred mainly on the problem of 'the gold reserves', in which the joint-stock bankers were particularly interested. The issue had been kept before the financial community especially by the efforts of two joint-stock bankers, Felix Schuster, governor of the Union Bank of London, and E. H. Holden, the assertive managing director (and from 1908 chairman) of the London, City and Midland Bank and the most spectacular figure in the amalgamation movement.[1] The nominal question that Schuster and Holden were raising was a practical one: how might the gold reserves be increased? But it could hardly be concealed that wider issues were at stake or that the problem existed because the arrangements prescribed in 1844 were no longer adequate. Whatever the merits of the Bank Charter Act, it had evidently not ensured the build-up of gold stocks as Britain's international commitments and the liabilities of the banking system expanded; and as Schuster and others repeatedly pointed out, the Act took no real account of the cheque-system which had developed so extensively since 1844.

Still more important was the fact that bankers and others were concerned about the gold reserves because they disliked the comparative frequency and severity of changes in bank rate in Britain, and the relatively high rate at which it was maintained. 'We did not want dear money or violent fluctuations in either direction', Schuster told the Union Bank's shareholders in 1901. 'On the whole a return to that condition when our money

---

[1] On the gold reserves controversy, and Schuster's and Holden's contributions to it, cf. J. H. Clapham, *The Bank of England*, Vol. II, Cambridge (1944), pp. 366–7, 379–82, 387–90 and 413–5; and T. E. Gregory's 'Introduction' to his *Select Statutes, Documents and Reports Relating to British Banking, 1832–1928* (1929), Vol. I, p. xxxix *ff*. Both Schuster and Holden referred to the matter repeatedly in their addresses to their banks' shareholders. Schuster gave considered statements of his views in a pamphlet, *The Bank of England and the State*, (Manchester, 1906), and a lecture to the Institute of Bankers (reported in the Institute's *Journal*, Vol. 28, pp. 1–22). Vol. 94 of the *Bankers' Magazine*, pp. 764–74, reprinted an address by Holden which was a good sample of his pre-1914 thinking; but as related in the text below, he later changed his mind on important issues.

market was the cheapest in the world would be best adapted to promote trade and secure our position.'[1] His point was a familiar one. The sensitivity of bank rate to overseas developments, and the roots of that sensitivity in the structure of the financial system, were the principal themes of (for example) R. H. Inglis Palgrave's *Bank Rate and the Money Market* (1903), and of many of his articles. Larger reserves were desired because it was believed that they would give the Bank more room to manoeuvre when it was losing gold. It is clear that when interest in the reserves problem flared up among bankers in 1907, the immediate cause was a belief that the rise of bank rate to 6 per cent in the previous autumn had not been justified by the state of the British economy, but was entirely a response to conditions generated abroad.[2] In addition to this line of criticism, there was another (which can be traced back at least to the Baring crisis and to Goschen's well-known suggestions for reform) that the Bank Charter Act was too rigid when a crisis threatened. This was expressed in a continuing interest in the provisions in German banking law for an emergency issue of currency when the banks faced a crisis, and in similar devices.

The sense of dissatisfaction with existing arrangements did not lead immediately to an extensive programme of reform. Schuster always favoured amendments, but comparatively minor amendments, to the 1844 Act; he held consistently that reserves were the vital issue, and that these must be built up before it would be safe to introduce more flexibility into the system. In 1906, a few cryptic remarks by the Chancellor (Asquith) set off rumours that a committee was to be appointed to examine the Bank Charter Act and recommend changes; but Asquith soon retreated.[3] However, as the discussion continued, bolder attitudes began to emerge. The principal innovator was Holden, and he continued to develop his ideas up to 1918.

At first Holden had believed that his objectives could be achieved within the existing legislation. By the beginning of

[1] *Bankers' Magazine*, Vol. 71 (1901), p. 324.
[2] The relevant passages in the speeches of the banks' chairmen in that year were printed together in the *Bankers' Magazine*, Vol. 83, pp. 423–7.
[3] *Bankers' Magazine*, Vol. 82 (1906), p. 5 and p. 65.

1914 he had grown more sceptical and was advocating a commission of inquiry into the financial system, and explicit provision in the Bank Charter for an emergency issue of currency when a crisis threatened.[1] (He later claimed that 'a committee of three bankers' submitted this proposal to the clearing bankers, that they had approved it, and that its adoption was only frustrated by the opposition of the Bank of England and then by the outbreak of the war.[2]) By 1918 he had come to favour a distinctly more radical revision of the Act, especially the abandonment of the balance-sheet distinction between the Issue Department and the Banking Department of the Bank, and replacement of the existing system of note-issue by arrangements which permitted the issue of notes 'on the security of bills of exchange and on the cash balance, so that a relation is established between the notes issued and the discounts'.[3]

As *The Times* and the *Bankers' Magazine* recognized the Cunliffe Committee paid little heed to these proposals, or to the line of reasoning out of which they had sprung. Nowhere was it more conservative than in its attitude to the Bank Charter Act and the note issue.[4] Holden it brushed aside with barely a mention. It is hardly surprising that the report should have provoked the 'destructive criticism' to which the *Bankers' Magazine* referred.

As Holden had been the most thoroughgoing reformer, so he was the most outspoken critic. His attack on the Cunliffe Report was the principal theme of his address to his bank's shareholders in January 1919. (Since he had last spoken to them he had completed his masterstroke, the absorption of the London Joint Stock Bank, which made the 'Midland' the largest bank in the world; but almost simultaneously his activities were officially condemned, by implication, in the report of the Colwyn Committee on Bank Amalgamation.) He complained that 'the Currency Committee have stated in effect that they cannot recommend anything better than the old system. They simply put us back to the old machine which has

---

[1] *Bankers' Magazine*, Vol. 97 (1914), p. 475.
[2] *Bankers' Magazine*, Vol. 99 (1915), p. 494.
[3] *The Economist*, (2 February, 1918), p. 171.
[4] Cf. Gregory, op. cit., p. lvi.

broken down before and which may break down again.' He repeated the familiar points about the rigidity of the Bank Charter Act, its inability to provide for emergencies, the size and frequency of the changes in bank rate that it obliged the authorities to make, and the adverse effect of these on Britain's competitive position. And he allied himself firmly with those who objected to deflation and high interest rates 'when the country is reconstructing its trade and industry, and when manufacturers and others are requiring increased accommodation.' The general tendency of his argument was to give first priority to domestic economic activity, and to identify reliance on bank rate and an inflexible note issue as sources of danger to the domestic economy.[1]

Holden's comments provoked a good deal of interest, but they did not lead directly to a general campaign against the Cunliffe Report. Holden died in the following July; Schuster, whose German background and connection had placed him in a rather difficult position during the war, was no longer a bank chairman, because the Union Bank had been absorbed by the National Provincial, and the chairman of the combined institution (Lord Inchcape) had been a member of the Cunliffe Committee; complaints against deflation voiced on behalf of merchants and manufacturers appeared a little hollow after the Cunliffe Committee's recommendations had been enthusiastically seconded by the Vassar-Smith Committee on Financial Facilities, on which trade and industry were strongly represented; and fears of deflation appeared irrelevant as the economy passed into the post-war boom which was nourished by a rapid expansion of bank credit.

But criticism did not altogether cease after Holden's death, and it soon found new material on which to fasten. F. C. Goodenough, the chairman of Barclays, maintained the pre-war tradition of hostility to the 'rigidity' of the Bank Charter Act by campaigning in favour of a note issue based on a gold reserve ratio. 'Experience has now shown', he was able to argue early in 1920, 'that the first recommendation of the Cunliffe Committee, advocating that every pound of currency created after a certain date should be covered by gold, is one

---

[1] His attack on the Cunliffe Report was reported in full in *The Economist*, (1 February, 1919), pp. 145-7.

that could not be carried into effect without great risk.'[1] By that time others who had initially welcomed the Report were ready to take the same line. The developments of the past year had prompted in some quarters a feeling that the conditions of the post-war economy were so abnormal that it would be both ineffective and dangerous to rely on the methods of adjustment recommended in the Committee's Interim Report. This attitude was strengthened by the Final Report. Some potential critics of the first report had held back because they hoped that the second report would go on from the statement of general principles to a discussion of detailed issues and current problems. The Committee's refusal to do so produced therefore a sense of anti-climax and complaints that it had shied away from the task of putting together 'a report of a more practical character'.[2] Accordingly, *The Economist*, for example, proceeded to advise the Government to disregard the approach (essentially the use of bank rate) which the Cunliffe Committee might be thought to have recommended, and to look around for measures which would be appropriate in the existing circumstances.[3]

The passage of time did nothing to weaken *The Economist*'s convictions on this matter, and it converted some others to the same view. In later years dissatisfaction crystallized in campaigns aimed at persuading the Government to appoint a new committee, which would consider the same issues as the Cunliffe Committee and which would be able to take into account the conditions which had developed since 1918. The most active part in these was played by the F.B.I., which approached the Government with formal requests for the appointment of a committee in 1921, 1923 and 1924, and at other times kept the issue alive in its journal.[4] Its demands for a new inquiry were

[1] *Bankers' Magazine*, Vol. 109 (1920), p. 249.

[2] *The Times*, in a leading article (15 December, 1919) headed 'Ridiculus Mus'.

[3] *The Economist*'s view of the second report (in its issue of 20 December, 1919, p. 1127) was not particularly hostile. But it went on to define its attitude more fully in controversies with Pigou (27 December, p. 1191) and Cannan (especially 17 January, 1920, p. 92).

[4] The memoranda submitted by the F.B.I. to the Government on these occasions were reprinted in its *Bulletin* (see the issues of 19 July, 1921, pp. 437–8; 31 July, 1923, p. 480; and 5 August, 1924, p. 445). One of the devices used to keep the issue before the Federation's members was to reproduce references to it from other sources, such as those referred to in the next footnote.

seconded by *The Economist*, and sometimes by others.[1] More generally, the diminished authority of the Cunliffe Committee is to be seen in the considerable scepticism with which bank rate was viewed between 1919 and 1924 as a means of restoring equilibrium in the post-war foreign exchanges.

THE BANK RATE AND DEFLATION

Holden's views were quoted at some length above because they were the forerunner of a more extensive and sustained attack on deflation in the following years. The beginnings of this attack can be located with some precision in November 1919, when bank rate was raised from 5 per cent to 6 per cent.

As Professor Morgan has pointed out in his *Studies in British Financial Policy*, the situation in the foreign exchange markets in October 1919 was one 'which by all accepted standards demanded a rise in bank rate'.[2] Yet when the Bank acted it was strongly attacked, and its critics included *The Economist* and the *Statist* which might have been expected to approve action based on such criteria. The existence of opposition was less important than the arguments on which it was based. 'Will a rise in bank rate check speculation more than it checks production?' asked *The Economist*. 'In view of the airy *insouciance* of the speculator as opposed to the plodding prudence of the producer, there is reason to doubt', it replied to its own question. It went on to argue that the current problems of high prices and inflated money supply had their origin not in speculation and an undue expansion of bank credit (which it regarded as the proper targets for the orthodox weapons of monetary policy), but in the wartime growth of the Government's floating debt. The only possible remedy, it argued, lay outside monetary policy in the narrow sense, in the Government's own tax and expendi-

[1] *The Economist*, (28 July, 1923, p. 137; and 23 February, 1924, p. 410). Among other demands for a new inquiry which the F.B.I. *Bulletin* reported were those voiced by the *Times Trade Supplement* for 1921 (which claimed that the 'findings' of the Cunliffe Committee were being fairly generally 'called in question'); by Oswald Falk (presumably Mr O. T. Falk, friend and for many years a business associate of Keynes) addressing the Royal Society of Arts; and by the National Council of the Pottery Industry (acting independently of the F.B.I. in 1922 and again in 1923). See the F.B.I. *Bulletin* for 6 December, 1921, p. 716; 21 March, 1922, p. 173; and 30 October, 1923, p. 667.
[2] E. V. Morgan, *Studies in British Financial Policy, 1914–1925*, (1952) p. 204.

ture policies.[1] These arguments (which closely resembled those that were advanced by the *Statist*[2]) formed the basis of *The Economist*'s later dissatisfaction with the Cunliffe Committee. They formed, too, the starting-point for its disagreements with Pigou and Cannan, but in its brief controversy with these two economists it introduced another consideration which had important implications. It argued that inflation could also be eased if production were allowed to rise while the money supply remained stable. Since it believed that 'an immediate and violent restriction on credit' would be inimical to production, this point fortified the anti-deflationary tendency in its attitude.[3]

The Economist maintained its hostility to deliberate deflation through the banking system in the next few years. But in the meantime this theme had been taken up by another, and in some respects more significant, commentator – Reginald McKenna. On succeeding Holden as chairman of the Midland Bank in 1919, McKenna decided to adopt his predecessor's custom of using the address to shareholders at the Bank's annual meeting as an occasion for commenting on the broad issues of monetary policy. In practice these addresses became for the next five years full-dress statements of the case against deflation, the case which Holden had presented in embryonic form in 1919.

McKenna's addresses to his shareholders (with one exception, the 1923 speech, which was severely criticized on technical grounds) were later collected and published as a book, so it is unnecessary to give here a summary of what he said on each occasion. But his main themes must be noted. McKenna began by arguing (like *The Economist*) that in post-war circumstances bank rate was an ineffective weapon, partly because it did not strike at Government short-term borrowing and partly because it was appropriate only to 'speculative' inflation whereas the post-war economy was in the grip of 'monetary' inflation.[4] The second of his points was by far the more important, not only because it had a wider bearing on theory but also because he developed it in a fairly rigorous way. The distinguishing feature of monetary inflation as McKenna described it is that 'wages and contracts of all kinds are adjusted to

---

[1] 8 November, 1919, p. 850.   [2] *Statist*, (8 November, 1919), p. 1028.
[3] 17 January, 1920, pp. 91–2.
[4] R. McKenna, *Postwar Banking Policy: A Series of Addresses*, (1928), pp. 28–9.

new price levels, and fresh capital is embarked in business on this basis',[1] i.e. that the rise in prices has extended to the major inflexible elements of costs. In these circumstances, McKenna concluded, 'the first effect of an attempt to force down prices by monetary deflation must be to cause severe trade depression' and the 'social evils' of great unemployment.[2] He argued that financial policy should not be directed to purely monetary considerations but 'should be one which will stimulate production and trade'.[3] In general, he thought that this would be achieved by stability of internal prices, which he recommended to the authorities as their immediate target.[4]

It is of some historical interest that McKenna objected to a fall in prices because it would favour creditors at the expense of debtors, and that he believed monetary deflation would in the long run be self-defeating because the fall in prices would 'be checked by the restriction of output which follows upon falling prices'.[5] But his major theme was the impact of monetary measures on trade and employment. Nor was he content with warnings cast in general terms. He identified 'part at least of the trade depression and unemployment' in Britain as 'the evil consequences of deflation',[6] and in 1924 advocated more explicitly 'expansion of credit' as the policy 'imperatively needed when trade is depressed and unemployment general'.[7]

It would be interesting to know how much McKenna, even at this early stage, might have been directly influenced by Keynes. But even if it were true that he had not derived any of his ideas independently, the importance of his stand would not in any way be diminished. As chairman of one of the most important and dynamic of the joint-stock banks and as a former Chancellor of the Exchequer, McKenna could not be written off as a member of 'the young and ardent body of economists ... of which Mr Keynes is the brilliant leader.'[8] His views necessarily had considerable authority and they received attention and respect.

[1] Ibid., p. 30.   [2] Ibid., p. 34.   [3] Ibid., p. 35.

[4] Ibid., p. 38. 'Stability' was the general theme of his 1922 address.

[5] Both points were made in the suppressed 1923 address. This was reported in *The Economist*, (27 January, 1923), pp. 158–62.

[6] *Postwar Banking Policy*, pp. 38–9.   [7] Ibid., p. 87.

[8] Sir Charles Addis (a member of the Cunliffe Committee, and a director of the Bank of England) reported in the *Bankers' Magazine*, Vol. 117 (1924), p. 18.

F

Moreover there is a good deal of evidence that from 1921 onwards there were many others whose thoughts ran along the same lines. Towards the end of 1921, as was remarked, the F.B.I. began to grow restive about the monetary policy, and to attribute to deflation many of the difficulties manufacturers had encountered since the break in the boom in the summer of 1920; it remained anxious and dissatisfied from then until 1925 (and beyond). Among McKenna's fellow-bankers, Goodenough also argued sometimes (although much more cautiously) against deflation and in favour of stability; he went furthest in 1922 declaring then that 'a policy of monetary deflation, such as was intended under the Cunliffe Committee's Report has been found to be impracticable' and that 'although . . . it would be practicable on a full tide of prosperity . . . yet under actual post-war conditions it has not afforded a practicable working basis.'[1] But perhaps the best evidence of the 'disrepute' into which, according to McKenna, deflation had fallen by 1922 is to be found not in the statements of particular critics but in more general assessments. For example, the inclusion in the *Annual Register* for 1921 of a judgement that the authorities had pursued a 'too rigid financial policy' (by which it meant a bank rate kept too high for too long) suggests that a fairly substantial amount of criticism was being voiced at the time. In the same way, special significance attaches to references in the *Round Table* to the existence of public controversy over deflation during 1923, and to the considered judgement of that journal that

> while there is a very large body of opinion which wants to see the pound sterling again at par with gold, there are very few so far as we know, who publicly advocate in order to secure such a result an actively deflationary policy at this particular moment, leading to a further fall in prices, further depression of trade and commerce, and a further increase in the burden of the public debt.[2]

The *Round Table* advocated fairly consistently during the early 1920s the restoration of the gold standard at the pre-war

[1] Reported in *The Economist*, (28 January, 1922), p. 143.
[2] *Round Table*, Vol. XIV (1923), p. 28, cf., *The Economist*, (27 October, 1923) pp. 732–3 for a further reference to the controversy then proceeding.

sterling-gold parity. In the passage quoted above it was not indicating its acceptance of the position taken by McKenna or Keynes, but was attempting to come to terms with arguments which now commanded fairly wide support.

I think it is fairly clear, then, that criticism of deflation was not either in the depths of the slump or at other times confined to a small body of monetary economists; and that some of the criticism came from persons (or journals such as *The Economist*) of authority or influence. If dislike of deflation did not quite manage to become the orthodoxy of the time, it did at least grow to be a respectable heresy. Possibly the best comment on the situation is to be found in McKenna's experience in 1923, after Baldwin became Prime Minister for the first time. The strength of the attack directed by McKenna in 1922 and 1923 against the policy being pursued by the Treasury and the Bank did not deter Baldwin from offering him the Exchequer. But it afterwards proved impossible to find him a safe seat in the City though, as Sir James Grigg remarks, 'it is to be observed that one of the sitting members did in fact accept a peerage less than six months later.'[1]

DEFLATION AND THE RETURN TO GOLD

If dislike of deflation was as strong as I have suggested, why did not more people follow Keynes in rejecting the gold standard and why were there not stronger protests against the decision to return at the pre-war parity in April 1925? Why, for example, did McKenna (unlike Keynes) acquiesce, however reluctantly, in the decision?[2] There are several answers to these questions, and they are bound up with the way the different issues were thought at the time to be related.

One important factor was the point stressed by both Professor Morgan and Sir Henry Clay – the strength of feeling in favour of both the gold standard and pre-war parity. There was a feeling, in other words, that these were important objectives 'worth some sacrifices' as the *Round Table* put it.[3] So dislike of

[1] P. J. Grigg, *Prejudice and Judgment*, (1948) p. 118. Grigg himself does not suggest that City dislike of McKenna's views on monetary policy might have been an obstacle to his entry into Parliament.

[2] On McKenna's attitude in 1925, cf. Grigg, ibid., p. 184.

[3] Vol. XV (1925), p. 270.

deflation might be, and doubtless in some cases was, outweighed by a still stronger dislike of a situation in which there was no gold standard and sterling did not 'look the dollar in the face'. But there is reason to believe that these were not in fact the decisive considerations. Full acceptance in principle of the gold standard and pre-war parity did not guarantee approval of the efforts made to restore the system. And those who continued after the outset of the slump, to regard the pre-war standard as a practicable goal frequently made use of other arguments designed to show that deflation would be unnecessary or need be employed to only a marginal extent.

There can be little doubt that faith in the ultimate restoration of the gold standard was sustained because 'many people . . . hoped that America's large gold hoard would lead to a rise of prices across the Atlantic, and so bring the pound sterling back to parity without a fall of prices here.'[1] This argument was a very familiar one, used for example by McKenna, Goodenough and the *Round Table*.[2] It had the useful quality that it might be employed to support a case either for the gold standard or against deflation. But however employed, it served to weaken the connection between the gold standard and deflation, which Keynes was trying to establish.

The belief that the pressure of gold supplies would in fact lead to a rise in U.S. prices became increasingly implausible as time went on. But when its implausibility was beginning to be recognized (which seems not to have been before 1924) another argument had been found to reconcile a dislike of deflation with support for the gold standard. This was the proposition that the famous gap between U.S. and British prices was now very small. And in the end it was this, rather than the more abstract arguments about deflation *versus* devaluation, or the gold standard *versus* a managed currency, that proved decisive. As sterling approached its nominal gold value in the foreign exchange market, these other issues were set aside. The strengthening of sterling made the need for deflation seem increasingly remote. And the matter was settled by the advice of the Chamberlain (Bradbury) Committee that, although the real gap in

[1] *The Economist*, (14 June, 1924), p. 1190.
[2] McKenna, reported in *The Economist*, (27 January, 1923), p. 160. Goodenough, n *The Economist*, (28 January, 1922), p. 143. *Round Table*, Vol. XIV (1923), p. 35.

domestic prices was larger than the foreign exchange quotations might suggest, any fall required in British prices would be 'not very large'.[1] The importance of this assurance is sufficiently indicated by the prominence given to it by the Government when it announced its decision to restore the gold standard, and by the strength of the attack launched on it by Keynes in *The Economic Consequences of Mr Churchill*.

In short, then, support for the restoration of the gold standard and pre-war parity – either in principle, or immediately as in the early months of 1925 – was not based on a general belief that the effects of deflation were negligible or beneficial. It rested to a significant extent on a conviction that it was possible to restore and maintain the gold standard without deflating on any serious scale. On the other hand, Keynes found supporters among those who *were* convinced that the operation of the gold standard system would involve deflation, even though they fully accepted in principle the case for a return to gold at pre-war parity. This last combination of attitudes is well illustrated by the Federation of British Industries.

THE F.B.I. AND THE GOLD STANDARD

Since the role and attitude of the F.B.I. seem to have been overlooked or misunderstood by the authors I quoted at the beginning, I want to conclude with a brief account of the Federation's activities. In this context, 1921 marked an important turning-point.

The F.B.I. was still in its formative period in the 1920s. Its members had conflicting views and conflicting interests, and its officers were unsure of their authority and had little experience in developing and maintaining consistent policies on technical issues. If any single attitude united the members it was a dislike of high taxation and Government 'interference' and 'extravagance'. This led to an instinctive sympathy with the Cunliffe Committee's emphasis on retrenchment by the Government as the first requirement in policy. To some British manufacturers at least, an appreciation of sterling appeared desirable because it would mean a fall in the cost of imported (especially American) materials. At the same time manufacturers had no

[1] Cmd. 2393, paragraph 19.

liking for credit restrictions or falling prices of finished goods.

Faced with these difficulties, the Federation never achieved a policy on the gold standard to which it stuck unwaveringly or which summed up the views of all its members. Nevertheless I think it can be said that after the post-war boom gave way to slump, certain members of its executive committee did devise a fairly distinctive attitude and did manage to have it accepted at vital times as Federation policy.

The first considered statement of the attitude of the Federation was the memorandum in which it requested, in 1921, the appointment of a new committee to re-examine the issues dealt with by the Cunliffe Committee. However, at this stage the Federation was fairly circumspect in its expressions of opinion and was willing to say categorically neither that any attempt to restore the gold standard ought to be postponed or abandoned, nor that deflation was responsible for the existing slump. Nevertheless the possible connection between foreign exchange policy, deflation and the fall in employment and activity was the major theme of the memorandum and of the letters sent to the Prime Minister by the Federation.[1] A point emphasized by the Federation was that account must be taken of changes in prices and costs in other countries as well as Britain and that, as it argued in its rejoinder to Lloyd George (in October 1921) 'the rehabilitation of the foreign exchanges cannot be brought about by the establishment of currency on a sound basis in one country alone'.

It is probable that the moving spirit in the approach to the Government was W. Peter Rylands, President of the Federation in 1921. As it happened, as early as 1918 Rylands had held reservations about the use of monetary policy to bring Britain back to the gold standard. In evidence before the Committee on Financial Risks (one of the many 'reconstruction' committees set up by Lloyd George's wartime Coalition Government) he had argued that an attempt to bring prices down quickly by monetary action would be extremely damaging, because wages

---

[1] The Federation's memorandum was printed in the F.B.I. *Bulletin*, (19 July, 1921) pp. 437–8. The events leading up to the decision to approach the Government are reported in the issues for 22 June, p. 391, and 12 July, p. 419. The Government's reply is in the issue for 4 October, p. 579; and the Federation's reply in that for 18 October, p. 597.

had moved up with or ahead of prices and these could not easily be reduced[1] – an interesting foretaste of the arguments used later by himself and by others such as Keynes and McKenna.

After Lloyd George rejected the Federation's representations in September 1921, Rylands sponsored the preparation and despatch to the Government of another memorandum which, while it dealt with a number of other matters as well as deflation and foreign exchange, was a little more forthright on the currency question. 'So far as trade . . . is concerned' it stated, 'it is important to remember that stability is of far greater importance than the re-establishment of any pre-war ratio with gold or any other standard of value. From this point of view, deflation can be as potent a source of instability as inflation.'[2] During the remaining few weeks of his term as president of the Federation, Rylands continued to attack the policy of re-establishing the pre-war value of sterling at the cost of internal deflation. He argued along these lines in a formal address to Scottish members of the Federation (a regular event in the F.B.I.'s calendar) and then at greater length at the Annual General Meeting of the organization. 'Instability of exchange is a very serious matter for manufacturers', he said on the latter occasion. 'We have got accustomed to a relationship between the "Bradbury" and the gold dollar of about four dollars to the pound, and I feel that the interests of the manufacturers would be best served if it could by some means be fixed at four dollars to the pound and remain there for all time.'[3]

By a mischance another part of this speech seriously impaired Rylands' prestige in the Federation and, although he continued to play a part in its affairs as a past president, he was less able to influence its policies.[4] Perhaps for this reason, less interest was

[1] Rylands was giving evidence before the Committee (which reported in Cd. 9224) as a representative of the F.B.I., but he stated that he was expressing his own opinion on this issue. His evidence has been preserved in Box 20 of the papers of the Ministry of Reconstruction, access to which is controlled by the Treasury.

[2] The memorandum was printed as an 'Economic Supplement' to the F.B.I. *Bulletin* of 18 October, 1921. The same issue contained an account of the steps leading to the despatch of the memorandum.

[3] F.B.I. *Bulletin*, (29 November, 1921) p. 696.

[4] In his speech, which was supplementary to the formal presidential address, Rylands dealt also with reparations. He put forward some imaginative proposals

shown in financial policy in the next few months. (Another reason may have been the strong and sustained rise in sterling which began at the end of 1921, and was accompanied by a series of reductions in bank rate which brought it from 5 per cent to 3 per cent in the first half of 1922.) However, the matter was raised again late in 1922 by Rylands' successor (O. C. Armstrong) who in his Presidential Address repeated both the demand for a new inquiry and the denunciation of 'the policy of deflation which the Government adopted in accordance with the recommendation of the Cunliffe Committee.'[1]

Armstrong (although no longer president) took the initiative again in July 1923 when he sponsored the preparation of another memorandum which was sent to the Government. (The meeting which approved his proposal was notable for an attack on 'Treasury theories of monetary policy' by Sir Alfred Mond, who in 1925 was one of the very few Members of Parliament to criticize the final decision to return to gold.[2]) From that time onward the issue remained almost continuously on the agenda of the managing committees of the Federation. The concrete results were formal submissions to the Government in October 1923, February 1924, July 1924 and finally in March 1925. These were supplemented by the flow of comment in the F.B.I. *Bulletin*, as well as in references in public speeches made by the Federation's officers.

For the most part the later submissions covered much the same ground as the 1921 memorandum, but there was a marked shift in emphasis in July 1924. From then on the Federation was committed to the gold standard as an ultimate objective and was no longer prepared to argue (as Rylands had argued in 1921) that the pre-war parity ought to be rejected as a goal. Indeed,

---

to solve the 'transfer problem' but these were felt by some of the Federation's members, especially in its Electrical Engineering Group, to conflict with their interests. They protested, and the Grand Council of the Federation had formally to repudiate Rylands' proposals. The episode and its significance are discussed briefly in C. B. Tennyson, *Stars and Markets*, (1957) pp. 146–7.

[1] F.B.I. *Bulletin*, (19 December, 1922) p. 880. Armstrong had previously secured the appointment of a committee of F.B.I. notables (including Rylands) to consider again the problem of the 'depreciated exchanges'. Ibid., 17 October, p. 712, and 31 October, p. 733.)

[2] F.B.I. *Bulletin*, (24 July, 1923) p. 466.

by March 1925 it was admitting that 'return of the pound sterling to parity with the dollar is an essential preliminary to a return to a gold standard by this country.'[1] But this did not reconcile the Federation to the idea that either the gold standard or deflation might be appropriate in the immediate future, for it had at the same time come to place more weight on the gap between U.S. and British prices and costs, and on the rigidity of British costs. In its memorandum of July 1924 it assessed the gap between prices in the two countries, as Keynes did, at about 10 per cent, and argued prophetically that the result of an attempt to eliminate the gap would be 'severe industrial friction and dislocation, brought about by the fact that, in order that goods may be produced at the new lower level, all the items entering into the cost of production, including wages and salaries, must be adjusted to this level.'[2] That the pound sterling was over-valued in foreign exchange markets, and that action to bring it to and hold it at parity would increase the disparity and 'make *permanent* what till then was only a temporary over-valuation', continued to be an important theme in the economic comment in *British Industries* until the Government's decision was announced in April 1925.[3]

In view of this record of opposition to deflation, and of rejection of comforting advice that the problem to be surmounted was 'not large', it would have been surprising if the Federation had actually welcomed the Government's decision. In fact its chief spokesman, the President of the Federation (Col. Willey) gave the decision anything but a warm welcome. He did remark that Britain's action should encourage other countries to follow its example, but he more than offset this with opinions which reproduced fairly faithfully the arguments that the Federation had recently been pressing on the Government:

---

[1] *British Industries* (i.e. the F.B.I. *Bulletin*, renamed in October 1924) (24 March, 1925) p. 222. Professor R. S. Sayers has suggested (in *Studies in the Industrial Revolution*, ed. L. S. Pressnell, (1960) p. 316, and reprinted in this volume as Essay 4) that in this memorandum the F.B.I. was 'advocating the restoration of the gold standard'. As I interpret it, the F.B.I. had come to accept that restoration was inevitable, but was pleading for action (a quick decision and international co-operation) to ease the equally inevitable hardships.

[2] F.B.I. *Bulletin*, (15 July, 1924) p. 406.

[3] *British Industries*, (30 April, 1925) 'Economic Supplement', p. x. Cf., the Economic Supplement (pp. vii–ix) to the issue of 20 January, 1925.

From the long point of view the decision is to be welcomed, but the immediate effect may create difficulties. At the present moment the pound is over-valued in relation to the dollar – i.e. in relation to gold. The relative price levels here and in America show this clearly. If, therefore, there is not a rise in American prices between now and 31 December which would wipe out this difference, there will have to be a corresponding readjustment downwards in the British price level ... [this] will involve a series of difficult readjustments in wage rates which it is hoped, may be avoided. It is to be assumed that the announcement made today, together with the powers given to the Bank of England, will rapidly bring the pound to parity with the dollar and will, for a time at least, increase the present difficulties of our export trade, which is already suffering from a greater rise in the value of the pound than is justified by the relative level of sterling and gold prices.[1]

In short, the Federation looked on the return to the gold standard with considerable apprehension, fearing that it would impose new burdens on British industry and would lead to a period of industrial strife as industrialists attempted to shift some of the burdens on to their employees. In this respect at least, despite its failure to accept either the case for a managed currency or any alternative to the pre-war parity, its assessment of the situation seems not to have been very different from Keynes's.

CONCLUSION

In his writings on monetary policy and the gold standard during and after the 1920s, Keynes sought to establish, from a distinctive and original theoretical position, that Britain must choose between the pre-war gold standard and internal stability, between deflation and domestic prosperity. In practice Britain chose the gold standard; Keynes's arguments were unavailing. As we look back on the decision at a distance of nearly forty years it is tempting to assume that Keynes was fighting a lone battle and that, among those who had opinions on the matter,

[1] *The Times*, (29 April, 1925).

deflation was judged a worthwhile or negligible price to pay for the gold standard, i.e. that the decision involved a conscious choice between the alternatives posed by Keynes.

I have tried to show that such an interpretation or reconstruction must be qualified in at least two of its aspects. Besides Keynes there were other, not unimportant, opponents and critics of the decision to return to the gold standard, notably the Federation of British Industries. And there was a much broader hostility to deflation, based on a fairly widespread recognition that it involved the depression of trade and employment. The Bank and the Treasury, far from commanding universal support for a policy of deflation, had to withstand almost continual harassment from a varied group of critics some of whom were men of influence and authority in financial matters.

When the issue had to be faced in 1925, advocates and opponents of a return to the gold standard could not be grouped according to their attitudes to deflation as a policy. At least as important was the division between those who did and those who did not believe that the pound would be over-valued at parity. The practical question at that time was not whether deflation was desirable but whether it was or would be necessary. Keynes's failure to win more converts to his stance of opposition was a reflection of his failure to convince his audience that the gold standard and deflation were, in existing circumstances, inevitably linked.

7 Trade Union Reactions to the Economic Crisis

SIDNEY POLLARD

[This article was first published in the *Journal of Contemporary History*, Vol. IV, No. 4 (October 1969).]

The trade unions in Britain, like those in the majority of European states, had long before 1929 become associated with a political party of socialist leanings. In this country the immediate reason for this association had been the hope of political influence and a share in the law-making power, rather than doctrinal support, but here, too, the unions had a right to expect some economic insight, and a guide line to the major economic events and policies, from their allied political wing. In this they were to be disappointed. When the crisis of 1929 struck and was followed by mass unemployment, the Labour Party and those union leaders who had been converted to socialism merely reacted by blaming capitalism in general, and reiterating that only socialism could effect a cure. A similar position was also taken by the International Federation of Trade Unions (I.F.T.U.).[1] At a time when the Labour Government of 1929-31 became totally committed to reviving capitalism rather than burying it, such an attitude became an escape from reality rather than a blueprint for realistic policy: the belief in ultimate socialism became an excuse for not doing anything meanwhile.[2] Ernest Bevin dealt with this escapism in a characteristically blunt and revealing outburst: 'I know that I could be answered by the usual socialist philosophy', he said contemptuously on one occasion in 1931, 'but when you go

---

[1] See Report of the General Council of the T.U.C. (hereafter G.C.T.U.C.), *T.U.C. Report*, (1933) 109; *T.U.C. Report*, (1930) 287-8; ibid., (1931) 432. For I.F.T.U., see ibid., (1932) 125.

[2] See *T.U.C. Report*, (1930) 291; Robert Skidelsky, *Politicians and the Slump, The Labour Government of 1929-1931* (London, 1967).

on a Royal Commission you have to deal with facts as they are and the problem as it is.'[1]

In consequence of this confusion of thought within the Labour Party, much of the running was made by the trade unions. It was the trade unions, rather than the disorganized Parliamentary party, which opposed the economy cuts of August 1931, and did so with reasoned arguments; it was they who summoned the National Joint Council, for some time out of commission, which represented the Executive of the Labour Party and the Parliamentary party, as well as the G.C.T.U.C., in December 1931 on the grounds that the links with the Labour Party might be satisfactory in opposition, but were different when the party was in power.[2] Within the N.J.C., it was the trade union side again which insisted on debating the attitude of a future Labour Government to its civil service, and to another parliamentary minority situation; and it was the trade union side which initiated the major policy debates over nationalization, in which it persuaded the Labour Party to think in terms of public corporations rather than ministerial management, and to define the role of the unions within them.

For the purposes of this paper, which is mainly concerned with trade union attitudes to employment policies, it is most significant that it was the G.C.T.U.C. which put forward the most authoritative official pronouncement on unemployment that the labour movement was to produce, in a report initiated by the economic committee of the G.C.T.U.C., and submitted to the T.U.C. in 1931.[3] With all its weaknesses, this was a well argued document, particularly on the historical background to the crisis, and immeasurably superior in its economic understanding to anything that emanated from the Treasury or its orthodox economic supporters. Whatever its precise merit, it was symbolic of the fact that it was the unions who found themselves, at this critical time, giving some backbone to

[1] *T.U.C. Report*, (1931) 464.

[2] Memo of the G.C.T.U.C. of 21 January 1932 for submission to the second meeting of the N.J.C. on 26 January. Two years earlier, on 16 January, 1930, the Cabinet had agreed that MacDonald should meet the G.C.T.U.C. to explain the 'difficulties of the Government in giving effect to certain parts of the Labour Party's programme'. P.R.O., CAB. 23/63.

[3] Alan Bullock, *The Life and Times of Ernest Bevin*, I (London, 1960), 202 ff., 449–53, 486–8, 512.

Labour Party thinking, rather than taking their ideas ready-made from outside.

In the 1920s, and particularly in the latter half of the decade, the trade unions, together with other critics of the economic establishment, had to explain and deal with British stagnation and mass unemployment which were exceptional in an expanding and booming world economy. The key to this peculiarly British failure was sought along two connected lines: the issue of unemployment relief and public works along one route, and the issue of financial policy, deflation and the return to gold at the old parity, along the other.

Adequate relief was, of course, a basic demand which raised no controversy within the trade union world. It was well expressed by A. Hayday of the General and Municipal Workers, as member of a deputation to the Minister of Labour: 'It is a permanent obligation on the State to provide the willing workers with an adequate income if work is not available, and this income should take into account whatever dependants there might be.'[1]

But relief was only a last resort, and the 1920s were still optimistic about the alternative, the provision of public works. To some extent this was a carry-over from the pre-war movement of breaking out of the poor law and obliging the larger local authorities, at least, to provide work on necessary improvement schemes in depression years: total employment might not be raised, but in an age when the trade cycle was taken for granted, fluctuations might have been evened out by this means. In the face of the much larger, and more persistent unemployment of the 1920s, ideas were more sharply defined, and public works were thought of not merely as providing useful amenities and setting men to work in the short run; there also began to be some understanding of the employment multiplier, and of the idea that the creation of new purchasing power, *via* deficit finance, might permanently enlarge the total flow of employment available.[2]

[1] *T.U.C. Report*, (1930) 129.
[2] This paragraph is much indebted to Donald I. McKay, David J. C. Forsyth, David M. Kelly, 'The Discussion of Public Works Programmes, 1917–1935: Some Remarks on the Labour Movement's Contribution', *International Review of Social History*, (1966). See also the chronology of trade union action in National Joint Council, *Workless: A Social Tragedy*, (1933) 13.

There are some signs of the employment multiplier in the official T.U.C. proposals from 1922 onwards: the effects of the downward multiplier particularly seem to have been widely understood. But when socialist economists of all schools repeatedly stressed the benefits of increasing the purchasing power of the masses by the payment of wages to men on public works, they all came up against the orthodox dogma that to finance such works out of taxation would merely divert employment, and to finance them by borrowing and unbalancing the budget was a certain way of ruining the country. In May 1930 the Labour Cabinet (Lansbury dissenting) was still adamant that 'however much we may be criticized, we must not be rushed into shovelling out public money merely for the purpose of taking what must inevitably be a small number of people off the unemployed register to work which is no more remunerative and *much more expensive* than unemployment.'[1]

In point of fact, the 1928 Liberal programme, *Britain's Industrial Future*, which enjoys such prominence in the history of the development of 'Keynesian' employment policies, carefully underplayed the role of deficit finance at that time, and even Keynes himself failed to follow through his own brilliant defence of it. It is therefore not surprising that Labour did not take easily to those new ideas which are now seen to be imbedded in it, even though the plan as a whole was little more than a collection of Labour's own proposals from 1921 onward. The official Labour reply, indeed, denied not only the Keynesian assumptions, but even Labour's own earlier doctrines, by decrying the public works programme as lasting for only two years, after which unemployment would be as bad as ever.[2]

In view of this total domination of the 'Treasury' dogma, the originality of Oswald Mosley's Birmingham proposals, published as *Revolution by Reason* in 1925, is all the more remarkable. Setting out to combine socialist under-consumptionist economics with modern monetary theories, Mosley demonstrated

[1] P.R.O., CAB. 23/62, 8 May, 1930.
[2] J. M. Keynes and H. D. Henderson, *Can Lloyd George Do It* (1929), esp. 25, 34-5; Lloyd George, Marquess of Lothian, B. Seebohm Rowntree, *How to Tackle Unemployment* (London, 1930); *Labour's Reply to Lloyd George. How to Conquer Unemployment* (1929); Norman Angell, *Government and Unemployment* (? 1931), 12.

clearly that in less than full employment conditions (he estimated the economy to be working at 30 per cent below capacity), extra purchasing power would bring about not inflation, but fuller employment. Such expansion was within our grasp: 'the banks possess the power to give and to allocate purchasing power through the manipulation of the price level, which of recent years has been ruthlessly employed in favour of the rentier and against the producer.' However, to make sure that it would not be used to finance profiteering and speculation (as it was to be soon after in the United States), the new purchasing power should be released only in credits to working-class consumers, employed and unemployed alike. Further, it should be issued gradually to make sure that productive resources could grow in step with the demand, and when 'maximum production', or full employment, was reached, industry should be taxed in proportion to the subsidy paid out to the workers, thus at one and the same time shutting off the inflationary pressure and continuing to transfer resources from the rich to the poor. Such a programme was compatible with socialist planning and with a managed currency, but one managed in favour of the people rather than the bankers' gold standard.

The plan, however, remained an isolated *tour de force*. It is doubtful whether even John Strachey, who sought to popularize it, understood the mechanism proposed, though he anticipated another development by using a Keynesian identity of saving and investment. The new ideas contained in it were simply ignored, and in Mosley's own memorandum on unemployment policy of January 1930, circulated among members of the cabinet, they are kept well out of sight.[1]

The other line of approach, dealing with financial policy, proved much more fertile. It is by now widely accepted that Keynes's was not the only voice raised in opposition to the return to the old dollar parity in 1925, and to the deflation which had to precede and follow it.[2] By 1929, virtually every-

[1] A copy of the memorandum, together with supporting letters by Lansbury and Thomas Johnston is in the Cabinet Papers, P.R.O., CAB. 24/31. Cf. Skidelsky, 169–82, 404–8; Oswald Mosley, *The National Policy* (London, 1931), esp. 15–17; Robert Boothby, *The New Economy* (London, 1943), 56.

[2] L. J. Hume, 'The Gold Standard and Deflation: Issues and Attitudes in the Nineteen-Twenties', *Economica*, (30 August, 1963). (Essay 6 in this volume.)

one in the Labour world understood the link between the precarious gold standard and the Bank of England policy maintained for its sake, which limited credit and purchasing power and thereby cut output and employment. It is clear that the trade unions, since they suffered the most, were at least as bitterly opposed as were productive industry and the joint-stock banks to reparations, deflation, restrictions, and to their consequences: rising fixed-interest burdens and an unemployment rate of between one and one and a half million.[1]

The quest for 'rationalization', which dominated this period, became a search not only for progress in general, but for the least painful way of lowering costs within the framework of official policy. The Mond–Turner conferences arose out of this quest for rationalization at a time when each side of industry had acquired a healthy respect for the other and both were unwilling to engage in further hostilities. The result was a bargain, a promise by the unions not to obstruct the dismissal of workers or their replacement by capital, in return for a promise by the employers not to cut wages. In effect it was, at least in the short run, a compact directed against the public (who might suffer a smaller output and higher prices) and against the unemployed, those existing and those yet to be thrown out of work. But it is too often overlooked that the Mond–Turner conferences were also an attempt by the main victims to combine forces against the Treasury and the City which had done them such grievous harm by handicapping their exports, encouraging imports, and discouraging investment and employment. In the section on the 'Gold Reserve and its Relation to Industry', the interim report, adopted by the full conference of 4 July, 1928, demanded the assurance that in future 'industry will not be arrested by the lack of credit facilities (due to a shortage of gold) as soon as increased production becomes effective.' The conference therefore resolved 'that under the special conditions in which the gold standard operates at the present time we are not convinced that it is either practicable or desirable that the credit policy of the country should be determined

---

[1] See W. N. Ewer and Francis Williams, *The World Muddle* (London, 1932); Francis Williams, *Democracy and Finance* (London, 1932); G. D. H. Cole, *Gold, Credit and Employment* (London, 1930), ch. 1; Cole and Bevin, *The Crisis* (1931); Labour Party, *Study Guide 1: Banking and Finance* (1933); *Study Guide 2: The Financial Situation* (1933).

more or less automatically by gold movements as in pre-war days.'

This rank heresy was repeated in a later interim report adopted on 12 March, 1929 and incorporated in the final report of December 1930; it provided a major impetus to the appointment of the Macmillan Committee, which was to educate a whole generation not only of economists, but also of trade unionists, about the facts of life of the money market.[1] There was also a battery of related proposals, including loans ('trade facilities') to industry, special relief for the mining areas, a development fund to be accumulated by industry in good years and spent on financing work schemes in slumps, and plans to raise the school leaving age and lower the pensionable age.

In the course of the proceedings of the Macmillan Committee, Bevin became one of the most eager pupils of Keynes and went on in his turn to educate the rest of the trade union movement on the working of the City, the gold standard, and the consequences of the policies of the 1920s; he was helped in this by Citrine and Milne-Bailey.[2] It was this that generated in Bevin and the trade union leaders who followed him, that suspicion and hatred of the bankers who had caused so much needless misery to millions, and led them, particularly after the fall of the Labour Government in 1931, to demand a much more radical reorganization of society than they had been prepared to consider before. 'For years', Walter Citrine cried in 1931,

> we have been operating on the principle that the policy which has been followed since 1925 in this country, of contraction, contraction, contraction, deflation, deflation, deflation, must lead us all, if carried to its great conclusion, to economic disaster.

> You return to the gold standard in 1925 Bevin echoed him and you give a miner and mine-owner the job of adjusting industry. They do not know what has hit them. They have got to handle all the problems of a million men. I think that is where our trouble starts. If we had gone on the gold standard

---

[1] Conference on Industrial Reorganization and Industrial Relations (Mond–Turner Conference), *Interim Joint Reports* (1928, 1929) and *Final Report* (1930); E. Bevin, *Statement on Melchett-Turner Unemployment Report* (1929).

[2] Bullock, op. cit., 394 ff.; *T.U.C. Report*, (1931) 28 ff., 268 ff.

at the then ratio, I believe we should have been leading the world today. . . . The process of [bank rate] operation is probably the most ruthless that could ever be devised. . . . First, to bankrupt the businessman – in other words, to do what so many economists refer to as 'healthy bankruptcies' . . . and secondly, to increase unemployment to a point that by the sheer pressure of poverty you get the lower production costs that the financiers desire. That is really its function. . . . On the Economic Council for two years continually some of us urged that an honest devaluation was better than waiting to be pushed off, that we were making too many of our people suffer week in week out waiting for the inevitable to happen. . . . You can talk about socializing your railways and other things. Socialize your credit and the rest is comparatively easy.[1]

With the crisis of 1929, the nature of the unemployment problem was drastically changed. Instead of deriving from deliberate policies engineered in London which could be changed by political decision, the depression which began then and reached its lowest point in 1931–2 was in the nature of a world-wide elemental force which no one knew how to control. As it happened, all the natural instincts of the unions, such as the wish to create employment at all costs, to pay generous unemployment relief, to keep up wage rates and incomes, would have turned out to have been beneficial. Yet in practice they failed to make any impression on the orthodoxy of either the Labour or the National Government. Moreover, having absorbed the Keynesian criticisms of the policies of the 1920s too well, union spokesmen failed in the early 1930s, as they had in the 1920s, to break the final thought barrier to deficit financing.

Soon after the New York stock exchange crash it became clear that a new phase of the depression had opened. The Cabinet's attention was drawn to it by the Minister of Labour on 26 March, 1930,[2] and similar assumptions soon coloured trade

---

[1] *T.U.C. Report,* (1931) 81, 409; Bullock, 428, 483, 497.

[2] P.R.O., CAB. 23/63. Margaret Bondfield, the Minister, also confessed that the official British unemployment figures had become most misleading, but a suggestion that a Commons Committee should examine the meaning of these figures was turned down since 'the Cabinet felt that for political reasons [it] would not be prudent at the present time.'

union discussions. The proposals canvassed by the unions under these new conditions fall under two main headings: the reduction of unemployment by spreading the available work; and economic planning and the provision of public works. There was also some discussion on the price level and on protection, but in view of the contradictory advice given by economists at the time, no clarity could emerge from the trade unions either.

The raising of the school leaving age, and the provision of adequate pensions on earlier retirement, as means of providing work for men of working age, had been proposed from the early 1920s on and had been accepted by the Mond–Turner conferences as desirable. Now that the unemployment figures were climbing to new heights, quickly topping the $2\frac{1}{2}$ million mark, this seemed the only possible method for achieving a rapid and massive reduction of these numbers. It formed a main component of Bevin's *My Plan for 2,000,000 Workless* (1933) and was to be found in every major Labour Party and trade union proposal, some authors, indeed, being under the illusion that they were creating jobs rather than redistributing them.

Such a reduction in the potential labour force, together with the more realistic proposal to reduce the working week to, say, 40 hours, could be justified as a method of absorbing the rapid rise in productivity of the 1920s, which was also held responsible for technological unemployment, and while only a few maintained the fallacy that all technical advance caused unemployment because the machine replaced labour, yet in the experience of every trade unionist there were clear cases where the machine had done just that, and where, in the state of the market, the displaced labour had not been absorbed but had gone to swell the numbers on the dole.

Neither the raising of the school-leaving age nor the more generous provision of old-age pensions would have been very costly. In 1933, Colin Clark estimated these two items in Bevin's scheme to cost £80 million and to save on unemployment and poor law assistance £50 million, leaving a net cost of only £30 million, not all of which would have to be met by the state.[1] By contrast, the compulsory reduction of hours might lead to

[1] Bullock, 517; for different calculations, see William Mellor, *The Claim of the Unemployed* (1933), 5–6.

costs of a different order of magnitude, at least if, as was widely demanded, it were to occur *without* loss of wages. Besides, the cost would have to be met by the private employer.

However, the raising of industrial costs in Britain would have run counter to all the existing policies, unless it were done by international collaboration, and the British trade unions were among the most active, between 1932 and 1934, first in the I.F.T.U. and then in the I.L.O., to get a convention on a 40-hour week ratified. The employers, however, remained bitterly opposed, and since most Governments, including the British, were at best lukewarm, the final text was weak and of little consequence. As a result, despite persistent and enthusiastic trade union backing, and the widely supported idea that greater leisure was a legitimate way of absorbing higher productivity and might in turn lead to the creation of new industries, no progress was made with any legal limitation of hours in Britain, except in the coal mines, where it required no more than an amendment to existing legislation. But the agitation left its mark, and in the better years of the mid-1930s, the shorter working week figured prominently among trade union demands.[1]

Among the numerous advocates of the shorter working week as a remedy for unemployment there were a few who came close to the thought barrier about expanding employment by creating new purchasing power. But again they came up against the self-contained thought system of orthodox economics. In order to defeat it, they would have had to build an equally complete one in reply, and none emerged until Keynes's *General Theory* in 1936. Thus the attacks of the heretics resemble short, sharp forays followed by quick retreats back to the sheltering walls of orthodoxy or obscurity, rather than a sustained campaign.

Some of the British delegates to the I.L.O., for example, including Margaret Bondfield, Minister of Labour in 1929–31, were much impressed by Giovanni Agnelli of the Fiat Company who had suggested on behalf of the Italian delegation that wages should be raised and purchasing power increased, rather

---

[1] Lord Melchett, *The Economics of Unemployment* (1933), 4; *T.U.C. Report*, (1932) 123–6, 412–20; (1933) 71, 160–4, 243 ff.; (1934) 278 ff.; (1936) 340–4; Bevin, *My Plan*, 8; Michael Stewart, 'Hours of Labour', in G. D. H. Cole (ed.), *British Trade Unionism Today* (London, 1939).

than the reverse, to absorb the unemployed;[1] but away from Geneva, the full power of the idea was dissipated in the usual haze about finance without inflation. The Independent Labour Party's position of 'increasing mass purchasing by establishing a living wage' and 'meeting the increased productivity of rationalized industry through a shorter working week and raising the school-leaving age' was equally indefinite, but appeared to favour redistributive taxation rather than credit creation.[2] This latter also seemed to be in the minds of the G.C.T.U.C. when they met the Cabinet in the last crisis of 1931 before the split: an extension of public works, as long as these were in themselves useful, financed by increased direct taxation, the suspension of the Sinking Fund, and a possible revenue tariff.[3] At the T.U.C. congress in 1932 one union leader demanded control over banking and currency, and 'control of industry in the direction of creating a continually increasing purchasing power, and a continual increase of social services for the workers in order that the consumption of goods and the standard of living of the working class can be continually increased so as to keep pace with the potentialities of rationalization under public control of industry.'

The reduction of the working week from 47 to 40 hours, declared another delegate, would go beyond an equivalent increase in employment:

> That does not finish there. Every man is a consumer; every man is a market. Today, while the factories of the world are rotten with surplus capacity . . . every man is more important as a consumer than he is as a producer. The effect of employing more men is cumulative; it does not stop at the door of the factory as every new man signs on. The newly employed engineer eats more, buys more, wants more; and the more he buys, the more he eats, the more he wants, the greater the number of other workers he throws into employment. To save British industry, the markets for British goods must be increased.[4]

---

[1] *T.U.C. Report,* (1932) 412–13.

[2] Fenner Brockway, *A Socialist Plan for Unemployment* (1931).

[3] This was in direct opposition to the advice received from the Conservative leaders; P.R.O., CAB. 23/67, (19 and 21 August, 1931).

[4] *T.U.C. Report,* (1932), 412–15.

No one else took up this line of thought, however, and even such an acute critic of the Establishment as G. D. H. Cole was uncertain about such issues as the extent to which loans, rather than taxes, could finance public works to create new employment; the need to balance the budget; and the extent to which induced employment must be devoted to objects that would not compete with the products of private industry.[1] Certainly, Arthur Henderson, leading the attack on the National Government in September 1931, went out of his way to emphasize that 'it is an elementary principle of sound finance that budgets should be balanced, especially under normal conditions';[2] even the G.C.T.U.C. went no further than to assert that 'only the greatest possible increase in public expenditure for productive work in times of crisis can lessen the disproportion between the efficiency of the productive forces of the nation and the consumption which falls short of this'.[3]

Yet by the end of 1932 at the latest, all the bricks which went to make the Keynesian employment theory were available and could have been used by the unions, had they been minded to assemble them. Most of them are to be found in that remarkable publication, *What Everybody Wants to Know About Money*, written by nine Oxford economists under G. D. H. Cole's editorship in 1932 and published in 1933, in which authors of such diverse political views as Cole, Gaitskell, Colin Clark and Roy Harrod, dealt competently with the powers of the banks to create credit, the need for Government deficit financing to cure unemployment, the employment multiplier, and the notion that when many resources are idle, additional purchasing power will serve to bring them into play rather than to raise prices. Within the next year or two, these notions, jointly or singly, had found their way into numerous Labour Party and trade union publications, though by no means into all.

Nevertheless, the conversion of the trade unions to an unorthodox, expansive policy was due less to British doctrine than to the American example. It was the first large-scale measures of the New Deal which emboldened British unionists to demand

---

[1] *Gold, Credit and Employment* (London, 1930), 108, 163; *Economic Tracts for the Times* (London, 1932); *British Trade and Industry* (London, 1932), 30.

[2] *Labour and the Crisis*, (25 September, 1931).

[3] *T.U.C. Report*, (1931) 129.

similar action, both from the existing National Government and from a future Labour Government. At the T.U.C. Conference in 1933, the report of the American fraternal delegate electrified the audience. Citrine moved a resolution urging the British Government, like the American, to undertake public works 'financed by the use of the national credit'. The Government, he alleged, had no policy at all, and while its words were expansionist, its actions were deflationist.

> They were not aiming at stimulating demand and increasing purchasing power, which would inevitably be reflected in a recovery of the home market, but were pursuing a national form of ca'canny . . . despite the fact that today it would be true to say that nearly every reputable economist in the country was convinced that the moment had arrived when public expenditure of that kind should be undertaken.

The other aspect of policy, economic planning and public works, was one in which the unions made the most radically new departure, swinging sharply to the left under the impact of the Labour Government's collapse in 1931. Instead of the earlier 'right to maintenance', the unions now demanded the 'right to work'.[1] The vision of combining the re-employment of idle labour with a purposeful direction of industry in the interest of social usefulness, was sufficiently attractive to bring even industrialists and political Conservatives under its spell. Trade unionists were naturally even more inclined to dissociate themselves from the opportunism of the Labour Government of 1929–31, and to think in terms of a wholly new approach. Among the positive results of this reorientation were the new view on nationalized industries and the planning and investment role of the banks, and on a national investment board. Basically, however, the vision of a planned industry directed to social ends was as divorced, and as distracting, from reality in the 1930s as the less distinct visions of socialism had been in the 1920s.

So much for the attitude of the trade unions to national economic policies relating to unemployment. But this leaves a large

[1] Bullock, 449. It was implicit already in a resolution of 1930, *T.U.C. Report*, (1930) 287–91.

gap. Were not trade unionists aware, even before the theory of the close interdependence of wages and the state of employment had become fashionable, of the weakening of their bargaining position by the rapid growth of the 'reserve army of labour'? Certainly no union leader could ignore the fall in the membership, which amounted, for all unions, to 8⅓ million in 1920 but to only 4½ million in the early 1930s. Moreover, there seemed to be no sign that either the fall in paid-up membership or the rise in unemployment had reached its limit. Given this unprecedented weakening of the union bargaining position, both the avoidance of any drastic wage cuts and the absence of any panic on the part of the trade union leadership[1] seem quite remarkable. What gave the unions their power, and their confidence, at this most unfavourable period?

There were three major factors. First, the loss in membership was often more nominal than real. The authority of the trade union was little impaired even among those who had fallen out of membership or had never been in it, and this was so not only among the skilled trades. In view of the position achieved by the unions in the two decades before 1929, mass blacklegging was simply inconceivable at the workshop level in most trades and most towns, though there were many encroachments, especially on apprenticeship. The history of the breakaway Spencer union shows how unusual the circumstances had to be to make such a development possible, and even then the assault came from a counter-union rather than from non-unionists.[2]

Second, the experience of 1926 made most employers unwilling to risk another costly clash with the unions, even if they could be sure of ultimate victory. The mutual support of union leader and industrialist was carried over from the Mond–Turner meetings and their plans for rationalization into the period of galloping unemployment. The downward 'stickiness' of wages was accepted by industry long before it became evident also to the City and the Treasury, and when both sides of industry learnt that neither free trade nor the exchange rate was sacrosanct, they found in their manipulation a much less costly

---

[1] As confirmed both by the literature and in an interview by Lord Citrine with the author.

[2] J. B. Jeffreys, *The Story of the Engineers 1800–1945* (London, 1945), 205; Alan R. Griffin, *The Miners of Nottinghamshire 1914–1944* (London, 1962).

and painful method of dealing with the consequences of the depression than a battle over wages.

Thirdly, there was also the organization of the unemployed themselves. A few unions, particularly among the skilled men, succeeded in keeping some link with those of their members who had to suspend the payment of contributions when out of work, but for the millions on the unemployed register it was the National Unemployed Workers Movement which preserved their tactical and strategic link with the men still at work. Its rallies, its hunger marches, and its constant agitation were often put down simply as the work of its communist and other extreme left leadership. But in refusing to sanction any work or even retraining at less than union wages, it played its part in protecting trade union standards. The N.U.W.M., founded in 1921, collaborated with the T.U.C. in its early years, but later fell foul of the G.C.T.U.C., while the T.U.C.'s own attempts to bring into being an unemployed workers association of its own, begun experimentally in 1927 and supported from the centre, was a failure in terms of the labour market, though it provided some useful social facilities to the men concerned.[1] Nevertheless, this extremist element in the N.U.W.M., repudiated, ostracized, and ignored as it was by the official leadership, was a valuable component of the total defensive power of the trade unions, mainly by maintaining pressure on politicians over insurance and relief rates, but also by guarding the flanks against possible offensives by employers backed by Government.

When the employment figures began to improve from early 1933 on, when real wages continued to rise because of falling prices and interest rates, and union membership took a decided upward turn again, the tone of the debate on unemployment in the trade union world underwent a marked change. The unions had learnt to live with over one million registered unemployed in the 1920s; they now accommodated themselves to a figure twice that size. Rather like Keynes in a more general sense, they

---

[1] Wal Hannington, *The Problem of the Distressed Areas* (London, 1927), 86 ff.; *Unemployed Struggles, 1919–1936* (London, 1936); 'The Unemployed', in G. D. H. Cole (ed.), *British Trade Unionism Today* (London, 1939); G.C.T.U.C., *What the Trades Councils are Doing. Report of the 8th Annual Conference of Trades Councils.* (28 May, 1932).

proved that equilibrium was possible at almost any level of unemployment. Now, as trade improved, they went over to the offensive. There was renewed and vigorous pressure from the T.U.C. in 1936 to implement the 40-hour resolution passed by a large majority at the I.L.O. Some unions had been pressing for it since 1933. Others, including even the miners, claimed, and many received, wage increases. But the issue of unemployment as such disappeared from the forefront of their consciousness as soon as a floor had been reached and that level was shown to be bearable. Apart from the Special Areas, the subject also virtually disappeared from the agenda of the T.U.C. and of the congresses of individual unions.

The crisis had, in fact, remarkably little permanent effect on the status and power of the British trade unions. They had proved that they were now permanent institutions, with an influence beyond that of the simple market position of labour; but this had already been proved in 1926. The traumatic experience of 1929 and 1931 moved them sharply to the left, and made support for a planned socialist economy universal among the leadership, helping them to think their way through to the public corporation as the form which socialized industry should take. But at the same time, and at the concrete, practical level, they also discovered a common cause with their employers, and came to accept that a tolerable society might be achieved by 'managing' the nation's credit in the public interest, without the need of nationalizing all the means of production, distribution, and exchange. In the event, the former solution proved to be much nearer to the predilections of the trade union leadership than the latter: the crisis turned out to have converted its majority to Keynes rather than to Marx.

Select Bibliography

I *General Histories of the Period*

ASHWORTH, W. *An Economic History of England, 1870–1939* (1960).

MOWAT, C. L. *Britain Between the Wars, 1918–1940* (1955).

POLLARD, S. *The Development of the British Economy, 1914–1967* (1969).

SAYERS, R. S. *A History of Economic Change in England, 1880–1939* (1967).

YOUNGSON, A. J. *Britain's Economic Growth, 1920–1966* (1967).

II *Financial and Employment Policies for the Period as a Whole*

BEVERIDGE, W. H. *Unemployment* (1930).

BROWN, W. A. Jr *The International Gold Standard Reinterpreted, 1914–1934* (N.Y., 1940).

CLAY, HENRY *The Post-War Unemployment Problem* (1929).

EINZIG, PAUL *World Finance 1914–1935* (1935).

HANCOCK, K. J. 'Unemployment and the Economists in the 1920s', *Economica*, XXXVII, (1960).

HARRIS, S. E. *Monetary Problems of the British Empire* (N.Y., 1931).

KEYNES, J. M. *Essays in Persuasion* (1931).

MCKAY, DONALD I., FORSYTH, DAVID J. and KELLY, DAVID M. 'The Discussion of Public Works Programmes, 1917–1935: Some Remarks on the Labour Movement's Contribution', *Intern. Rev. for Social History* (1966).

ROBBINS, LIONEL *The Great Depression* (1934).

ROBERTSON, D. H. *Essays in Monetary Theory* (1940).

III *Biographies*

BOYLE, ANDREW *Montagu Norman. A Biography* (1967).

CHANDLER, L. V. *Benjamin Strong, Central Banker* (Washington, 1958).

CLAY, SIR HENRY *Lord Norman* (1957).

EINZIG, PAUL *Montagu Norman. A Study in Financial Statesmanship* (1932).

HARGRAVE, JOHN *Professor Skinner alias Montagu Norman* (1939).

HARRIS, SEYMOUR *John Maynard Keynes* (1955).

HARROD, ROY F. *The Life of John Maynard Keynes* (1951).

MOREAU, EMILE *Souvenirs d'un Gouverneur de la Banque de France* (Paris, 1954).

LEITH ROSS, SIR F. W. *Money Talks: Fifty Years of International Finance* (1968).

SCHACHT, HJALMAR *My First Seventy-Six Years* (1955).

WILLIAMS, FRANCIS *A Pattern of Rulers* (1965).

IV The Re-establishment of the Gold Standard

BROWN, W. A. Jr *England and the New Gold Standard, 1919–1926* (New Haven, 1929).

GREGORY, T. E. (ed.) *British Banking Statutes and Reports*, II, 1847–1928 (1929), (contains the Reports of 1919 and 1925).

GRIGG, SIR P. J. *Prejudice and Judgment* (1948).

MCKENNA, REGINALD *Post-War Banking Policy. A Series of Addresses* (1928).

MOGGRIDGE, D. E. *The Return to Gold, 1925. The Formation of Economic Policy and its Critics* (Cambridge, 1969).

MORGAN, E. VICTOR *Studies in British Financial Policy, 1914–25* (1952).

PIGOU, A. C. *Aspects of British Economic History, 1918–1925* (1947).

V The Gold Standard Years, 1925–31

CLARKE, STEPHEN O. V. *Central Bank Co-operation, 1924–31* (N.Y., 1967).

Committee on Finance and Industry (Macmillan Committee), *Report*, Cmd. 3897; *Evidence* (1931).

GREGORY, T. E. *The First Year of the Gold Standard* (1926).

HAWTREY, R. G. *The Gold Standard in Theory and Practice* (1927, 4th ed. 1939).

JONES, J. H. 'The Gold Standard', *Econ. J.* 43/172, (December, 1933).

MORGAN WEBB, SIR CHARLES *Ten Years of Currency Revolution* (1935).

WILLIAMS, DAVID 'Montagu Norman and Banking Policy in the Nineteen-Twenties', Yorks. *Bull. of Econ. and Soc. Research* XI, (July 1959).

WILLIAMS, JOHN H. *Post-War Monetary Plans, and Other Essays* (N. Y., 1944).

VI The Repeal of the Gold Standard and After

COLE, G. D. H. (ed.) *What Everybody Wants to Know about Money* (1933).

CRICK, W. F. 'British Monetary Policy, 1931–7', *Bankers' Magazine*, CXLV/1127, (February, 1938).

EINZIG, PAUL *The Tragedy of the Pound* (1932).

GREGORY, T. E. *The Gold Standard and its Future* (1931).

NEVIN, E. *The Mechanism of Cheap Money: a Study of British Monetary Policy, 1931–39* (Cardiff, 1955).

SKIDELSKY, ROBERT *Politicians and the Slump. The Labour Government of 1929–1931* (1967).

WILLIAMS, DAVID 'London and the 1931 Financial Crisis', *Econ. Hist. Rev.*, XV, (1963).